THE LEGAL JOB INTERVIEW

WINNING THE LAW-RELATED JOB IN TODAY'S MARKET

CLIFFORD ENNICO

KAPLAN PUBLISHING

New York

This publication is designed to provide accurate and authoritative information in regard to the subject matter covered. It is sold with the understanding that the publisher is not engaged in rendering legal, accounting, or other professional service. If legal advice or other expert assistance is required, the services of a competent professional should be sought.

Published by Kaplan Publishing, a division of Kaplan, Inc.
1 Liberty Plaza, 24th Floor
New York, NY 10006

Printed in the United States of America

Library of Congress Cataloging-in-Publication Data

Ennico, Clifford R.
  The legal job interview / by Cliff Ennico.
     p. cm.
  Includes bibliographical references and index.
  1. Law—Vocational guidance—United States. 2. Employment interviewing—United States. I. Title.
  KF297.E56 2008
  340.023'73—dc22   2008026607

2008
10 9 8 7 6 5 4 3 2 1

ISBN-13: 978-1-4277-9796-4

Kaplan Publishing books are available at special quantity discounts to use for sales promotions, employee premiums, or educational purposes. Please email our Special Sales Department to order or for more information at kaplanpublishing@kaplan.com, or write to Kaplan Publishing, 1 Liberty Plaza, 24th Floor, New York, NY 10006.

To my late father, Leonard W. Ennico (1922–2000),
the hero of my childhood.

CONTENTS

About the Author

C**LIFF ENNICO** (*www.cliffennico.com*) is widely considered to be one of America's leading experts on the legal problems facing entrepreneurs and privately owned businesses.

A native of Yonkers, New York, Ennico is best known as the former host of *MoneyHunt®*, the fast-paced **PBS** television series where entrepreneurs defended their business plans before America's toughest panel of business experts (*www.moneyhunt.com*), as well as its spin-off series, *MoneyHunt Small Business Challenge*™, which aired on over

100 PBS television stations during the 1990s and early 2000s. His weekly syndicated newspaper column, *Succeeding in Your Business*™, for which he is known as the "Ann Landers of the business world," appears in dozens of major newspapers and business websites throughout North America (*www.creators. com/lifestylefeatures/succeeding-in-your-business/succeeding-in-your-business.html*). He also hosts the legal and tax channel for the Small Business Television Network (*www.sbtv.com*) and is a frequent contributor to *Entrepreneur* and other small business magazines.

Ennico is the author of several books on entrepreneurship and small business management, including *MoneyHunt: 27 New Rules for Building a Breakaway Business* (HarperCollins, 2000) and *Small Business Survival Guide* (Adams Media, 2005), and he speaks nationwide to business and professional groups on issues facing entrepreneurs (*www.bookaspeaker.net/ searchDetail.asp?lastName=ennico&entryID=710*).

A member of the faculty of eBay University (*www.ebay. com/university*), Ennico speaks throughout the United States on ways to set up e-commerce businesses on eBay, the world's leading Internet auction site. He has authored two leading books on the U.S. legal and tax aspects of doing business on eBay, *The eBay Seller's Tax and Legal Answer Book* (AMACOM, 2007) and *The eBay Business Answer Book* (AMACOM, 2008).

As a lawyer, Ennico has represented over 15,000 corporations and other business entities in his 28-year career. Formerly associated with the New York City law firms of Willkie Farr & Gallagher and Thacher Proffitt & Wood, Ennico currently operates his own legal and business development consulting practice in Fairfield, Connecticut.

Throughout his career, Ennico has been a pioneering author in the field of legal career management. In addition to *The Legal Job Interview,* his books for law students and young lawyers include *Your Legal Career: Finding Success and Satisfaction in the Legal Profession;* and *Business Lawyer's Handbook: An Introduction to the Corporate Counsel's Life and Work* (*www.legalcareer.com*).

Ennico holds a BA degree, *magna cum laude,* from Dartmouth College and received his JD degree from Vanderbilt University School of Law, where he was articles editor of the *Vanderbilt Law Review.* He is a member of the Connecticut Bar Association, the New York State Bar Association, and the Fairfield County Bar Association.

Preface

"The more things change, the more they remain the same."
—Jean-Baptiste Alphonse Karr (1808–1890)

It never ceases to amaze me is how little things have changed when it comes to interviewing for a job in the American or Canadian legal profession. Mark Twain once quipped that when the end of the world occurs, he "wanted to be in [a certain city in the Midwestern United States], because things happen there 50 years later than they happen anywhere else." The same could be said of the way law firms, corporations, and government agencies go about hiring their legal talent. Here are some observations about the legal job search that are just as true today as they were in the 1990s:

- The vast majority of American law students have no clue what the legal profession is about—they have based their career choice upon television programs such as *Boston Legal*, novels about lawyers crusading for truth and justice, movies such as *Michael Clayton* (hey, if every lawyer looked like George Clooney...), or influential lawyer relatives who clearly have accentuated the positive and eliminated the negative in selling what they do to the next generation.
- There continues to be a dearth of information about how to succeed in the practice of law. The few books out there are written mostly by nonlawyers or "nonpracticing lawyers" (translation: law school graduates who couldn't find a job and so went into another line of work) who have not personally experienced the things they are writing about.
- While technology has transformed the way in which law is practiced and legal research is conducted, it has had little or no impact on the way law firms, corporations, and government agencies go about the hiring process. You still need to interview with a human being.
- While the business world has become a more casual, laid-back place, the legal profession still remains a bit, shall we say, stodgy? Lawyers still care deeply about professional image, reputation, and what one attorney friend of mine

referred to as "quiet competence." If your local clothing store still carries two- and three-piece suits, thank the local lawyers who are keeping those product lines in business.

Thus, in 2008, there still is a need for a book like *The Legal Job Interview*. This book is not just about interviewing for a legal job; it is about surviving as a legal professional at the dawn of the third millennium A.D. (or C.E. if you prefer).

I am delighted that Kaplan Publishing has taken up the mantle of providing a fresh perspective on career issues facing the legal profession. *The Legal Job Interview* is planned as the first in a series of books for law students, young lawyers (zero to five years in practice), and "lawyers in transition" of all ages to help them steer through the treacherous waters of a profession that is undergoing dramatic change—both in terms of the technology it is using and the role it is expected to play in American society.

I remain convinced that there is still much work to be done to help American lawyers find their way in the world. I am delighted that Kaplan Publishing shares that conviction, and I look forward to continuing what has become a labor of love in being one of the guideposts lawyers can use to become successful in their profession.

A book like this cannot succeed without the help of many people, many of whom (for reasons of confidentiality) must remain anonymous, but I am especially grateful to the following people:

Jennifer Farthing and Monica Lugo, my editor, at Kaplan Publishing, for believing in this project as well as the idea that a 54-year-old attorney still has something meaningful to say to younger generations of lawyers.

My former next-door neighbor and dear friend Gary Farber, who as a teenager was mowing my lawn when the first edition of *The Legal Job Interview* came about, and as a publishing executive today was instrumental in making the second edition possible.

My wife Dolores, who has endured each and every one of my own personal career transitions, and who has often had to "solo" at family gatherings because of my writing deadlines.

My late father Len Ennico (1922–2000), to whom this book is dedicated, and who taught me that a career is much more than a job.

The legions of lawyers who interviewed me and worked with me over the years, who have taught me more than any law school ever could about what really goes on in the legal profession.

Regarding the last of these, I hope that they are still employed.

Cliff Ennico
Fairfield, Connecticut
March 30, 2008

Chapter 1

The Subtle Art of Being Interviewed

A LAWYER'S CAREER PATH USED to be extremely predictable. He graduated from law school, he passed the bar in a state where he expected to live out the rest of his life, he apprenticed himself to a law firm as an associate or salaried employee, and he worked for the firm for five to seven years while developing his skills. At the end of the five to seven year apprenticeship period, he either was made a partner of the firm (which guaranteed him a job for life) or was passed over.

But being passed over still meant that he easily found a job as partner of a smaller firm in the same town or as in-house counsel to one of his firm's business clients. Settling into one of these positions, he then continued to practice law in his chosen specialty until his retirement or death.

Each step in this career path was very well defined. While some lawyers found this narrow track stifling, most found it quite comfortable, if not downright cozy. After all, lawyers are not normally inclined—and are certainly not trained—to take risks. The only practical choice for those who could not fit into one of the well-established legal career niches was to leave the practice of law entirely, and the list is long of those who have left the legal world for careers in entertainment, politics, government service, business, and the arts. Those who stayed in the profession had the luxury of never having to worry about their careers. Legal employers were careful to take care of their own, and clients seldom if ever changed lawyers.

The last decade saw dramatic changes in the lawyer's traditional career path. Corporations began hiring more lawyers as in-house counsel, in the hopes that by paying them a straight salary instead of an hourly billing rate, they could get a better handle on their spiraling legal costs. Many of these in-house legal departments have grown to rival in size and competence some of the largest and most prestigious law firms in the United States.

Also, many clients became increasingly loyal to individual attorneys whose judgment they respected, rather than to the firms. This shift in client loyalty eventually led savvy lawyers to recognize that if they changed employers, their clients would follow.

Law firms also became evermore subject to economic pressures, which led them to lay off partners who were not contributing to the firm's bottom line, retire their senior partners early, and fire associates and partners in areas of practice that were temporarily or permanently depressed.

The result of these dynamic changes is that the profession of law is no longer a cushy refuge from the realities of the business world. Today's lawyers and legal professionals can expect to change jobs, voluntarily or involuntarily, much more frequently than ever before. Mobility—from one type of legal environment to another, from one location to another, from one area of practice to another—is on the rise, leading to greater career insecurity and instability. Lawyers today have to spend a substantial amount of time planning their careers, refining those plans as their career unfolds, keeping their eyes open for changes in the legal environment that may make their current position no longer tenable, and making career transitions. At each stage of their careers, they will spend more time than ever before interviewing for jobs. This book is a guide to the special, and often unique, art of interviewing for a legal job.

Once upon a time, a lawyer was judged solely on the strength of his technical skills. The growing pressure on lawyers to become more attuned to the economics of practice compel them (in some cases against their will) to develop people skills—the abilities to communicate with others outside the profession, market themselves to prospective clients, deal with difficult people, achieve objectives through the work of others (which those outside the profession of law call management), and win friends and support without being idiosyncratic.

Interviewing skills are among the most crucial people skills that the young lawyer or legal professional must master in order to be successful. Lawyers are constantly interviewing—eliciting information from clients, persuading a client (or a colleague or a judge) to adopt their point of view, seeking a higher paying or more challenging job, or convincing their superiors that they are more capable than the person across the hall and therefore more deserving of partnership.

While this book focuses on the skills necessary to survive a legal job interview, interviewing (in the broadest sense of the word) does not stop when the job offer is made. The wise lawyer never stops interviewing and treats every interpersonal interaction on the job with the same care and caution as if it were in a formal interview situation. Simply put, successful lawyers and legal professionals always conduct themselves in such a way as to make the most positive possible impression upon those around them.

A WAR STORY, OR HOW I LEARNED TO STOP WORRYING AND LOVE THE LEGAL JOB INTERVIEW PROCESS

When I was seeking my first legal job more than two decades ago, I scoured the business and career sections of every bookstore in town and devoured every book and article I could find on the art of interviewing (even then there were quite a few). I believed that interviewing for a job required a certain amount of acting ability; I sensed that I could not simply be myself in an interview setting, and yet I was not sure exactly how a young lawyer just starting out should present himself.

I therefore looked to nonspecialized (i.e., not written for lawyers) books on interviewing for the answers.

I found, however, that even though I was following the rules and principles in these books to the letter, I was not having much success; in some cases it was painfully obvious that I was turning the interviewer off the minute I opened my mouth. At first I attributed this to my own lack of interviewing skill, which I thought would come in time, or to my own failure to prepare hard enough for the interview, which led me to triple the amount of time spent researching and analyzing prospective employers. All to no avail.

As the rejection letters continued to pile up in a big way, I began to realize that the skills taught in interviewing books were not helping me succeed in my goal of obtaining a legal job and that a fairly radical change in tactics would be necessary. I slowly began to realize that interviewing for a legal job was much, much different than interviewing for a job in business management, the media, government service, or any other occupation on Earth. Sadly, no book had then been written about the special tactics that would be necessary in a legal job interview (to my knowledge, this is the first book on the subject). I could not, of course, rely on words of wisdom I received from other law students; after all, they were my competition. Nor could I rely on advice from legal placement people of my acquaintance, since they themselves had never thought of legal job interviewing in a systematic way. They were referring me to the same general interviewing books whose approach I had rejected. Despite excellent credentials, I began to fear that I would never find a first job, much less learn these special tactics for the long run.

I then had an experience that changed my entire life and taught me in a single, Zen-like flash what it would take for me to succeed in a legal job interview. I had flown to New York City to interview with several major law firms. I had no difficulty obtaining interviews, so I knew my credentials were not the cause of my troubles. It was the last day before my flight back to law school, and I was scheduled to interview with two firms: I was to spend the morning at Firm A—a freewheeling, intense place known then for its antitrust work—and the afternoon at Firm B, a stuffy, white shoe firm that represented many of the old-line investment banking firms on Wall Street.

The morning at Firm A, I thought, went spectacularly well. I met three of the most interesting people I had ever met in my life, and they seemed to love me. We talked animatedly for a couple of hours, and then they invited me to lunch on the spur of the moment. Three of the firm's top partners took me to a restaurant that was a favorite haunt of movie and television stars, sports figures, and Wall Street executives. While there we went through three bottles of wine, and we regaled each other with war stories from our respective pasts (I had been a crime reporter for a daily newspaper before attending law school and could match them story for story). They wanted me to return to the firm and spend the rest of the day, but I told them I had to catch an early flight because of a law review deadline. (I couldn't tell them about the interview at Firm B!) When we left the restaurant, I thought I was a shoo-in to receive an offer from Firm A.

On the way to my afternoon interview at Firm B, I realized I was not in the best shape for an interview. The wine had made me much too mellow, and I started frantically chewing on breath mints so that this fact would not be too obvious. Even worse, I had gotten so caught up in Firm A's salesmanship that I completely forgot all the information I had gleaned in my extensive research of Firm B. I thought to myself, "Holy cow, Ennico! You can't go through an interview like this, especially with a stuffy place like Firm B that wants every hair in place. Maybe you should feign illness and ask for a postponement." Then, after a few minutes, I said to myself, "Hold on a minute. It's going to be weeks before you're back in town again. This may be your last chance for an interview at Firm B. Besides, Firm B is one of Wall Street's most elite law firms; someone with your background probably doesn't have a chance there anyway. You know you've got an offer from Firm A—you really knocked them dead—so you don't really need to try so hard with Firm B. Let's just go through the motions at Firm B and get on back to school."

Sure enough, Firm B was as stodgy as I had imagined; the office looked as if it had not been redecorated since the Eisenhower administration. To keep my lack of preparation hidden from view, I sat through a series of interviews with the firm's senior partners in almost total silence. I let them do all the talking (they seemed to like to hear themselves talk). On the rare occasion when they asked me a question or showed any interest at all in me, I thought for a moment, uttered a direct four- or five-word answer, and then countered with a question of my own, which started them off on another tangent for what seemed like hours.

As I left Firm B's offices, I said to myself, "Well, you can write that one off. You didn't give them much reason to be interested in you; you just sat there like a bump on a log. Oh well, at least you did well at Firm A."

The letters from Firm A and Firm B arrived the same day. The letter from Firm A was a form rejection letter, just like the dozens of others I'd received. I was crushed. I just couldn't believe I had blown it. Everything had seemed to go so smoothly, and everyone at Firm A seemed to think I was the greatest thing since sliced bread. I actually (this does not happen to me often) started to cry. Would there be no future for me in the law?

I almost did not open the letter from Firm B. It was in the same sort of envelope as the letter from Firm A, and I had always believed that if you were going to be made an offer it would come in a different sized envelope. Besides, hadn't I done a terrible job of interviewing at Firm B? The best I could have hoped to do was hide the fact that I was not prepared for my interview there; those breath mints could not have done the job. I almost threw the unopened letter in the garbage. Even today I can't recall what made me open it—I probably thought that it would complete my collection of rejection letters from New York law firms, which might be worth something to a collector.

The letter from Firm B was not a form letter. It was a personal letter written by the firm's most powerful partner (the autograph alone is probably worth some money today), inviting me to join Firm B as an associate, for a salary so astronomically high that at first I thought it was a typographical error.

I sat on my sofa bed in stunned silence. What in the world had I done wrong at Firm A, and what in the world had I done right at Firm B? Why were my perceptions of my own performance so off base? Why did I think I had wowed them at Firm A, when in fact I had turned them off? And why did I think I had made a fool of myself at Firm B, when in fact I gave the best performance of my career? The answer didn't hit me until later that night, after a raucous celebration at the law review for receiving the offer from Firm B.

The lessons I learned from that fateful day at Firm A and Firm B are the lessons I teach in this book so that you won't waste as much time as I did collecting rejection letters from law firms, corporate legal departments, and government agencies. This is a very personal book—an essay, not a treatise or textbook. It is not a book of absolute rules, but rather a summary of my own experience in legal job interviews and the lessons I have learned.

I have practiced law for almost three decades, in a variety of legal environments, and have made several successful career transitions using the interviewing skills that I have outlined in this book. When you interview for a legal position, your interviewer is not a personnel or human resources executive but rather a lawyer just like you (or just like you want to become). Lawyers are not trained in interviewing techniques, as personnel executives are, and so they often don't know the basic rules of interviewing job candidates. The results can often be amusing and sometimes tragic. In any event they are unpredictable.

One of the shortest interviews I ever had was with a large New York City law firm that had the reputation of being a sweatshop. The interviewer said nothing about the firm and asked only three questions: "Are you married?" "What were your billable hours last year?" and "When can you start?" The interviewer made me an offer immediately upon my giving the right answers to these questions ("No." "More than 2200 hours." "As early as next week."), and then left it up to me to figure out whether or not I wanted to work there (I didn't). Those three questions told me more about the firm's attitude toward associates than anything the interviewer could have *actually* told me.

At another interview, the law firm partner's office was bedecked with American flags of all sizes and shapes, including one covering an entire wall that looked as if it had flown over the White House at one time. The interviewer asked me questions covering virtually every facet of my personal and professional life and seemed satisfied with my answers until I made an offhand remark while answering a question about my summer jobs in college. I said, "I'm afraid I didn't have too many white-collar jobs when I was at college; the summer jobs I did have were more blue collar in nature." The partner scowled, jumped to his feet, banged his fist down hard on his desk—so hard that the flag on the wall became unhinged in one corner—and fixed an icy stare at me. I thought for a moment he was going to hit me. He then shouted through his clenched teeth in a voice I am sure every lawyer in the firm could hear, "M-I-S-T-E-R Ennico, the profession of law IS a blue-collar job. In fact, it is the most honorable blue-collar job in the United States of America. There is nothing white collar about it. Lawyers are the highest paid factory workers in this country. And don't you ever, ever forget that if you expect to work here, M-I-S-T-E-R Ennico!" Needless to say, I was not too keen on working there either.

You cannot anticipate what every interviewer will do in every legal job interview. The trick is to avoid getting into no-win situations with interviewers. For example, many know only too well that they don't have good job interviewing skills. If you can convince them that they can nevertheless make the right decision about you, you'll be in great shape. This is a lot easier than it appears at first. And remember, interviewing is not merely a job-hunting tool, but a career management device that you will employ virtually every day of your professional life. This book will provide the practical advice you need to help you refine this crucial career development tool.

SOME SPECIAL CONSIDERATIONS

You will note that I have not included a chapter just for women or minority candidates. While there is, sadly, still a good deal of stereotyping in the legal profession, I do not think there really is a different way of interviewing when you are a woman or a minority group member. The rules and techniques described in this book should work no matter who you are. In addition, spotting and dealing with discrimination in an interview situation is a topic that is very adequately treated in the books listed in the bibliography.

Finally, I have chosen to use the masculine pronoun throughout this book, rather than constantly providing both singular pronouns at the same time or balancing the use of each pronoun throughout the text. I ask that the reader look upon it as referring to both sexes. In the words of a legal document that once crossed my desk (and which thankfully I did not draft), "the use of the masculine gender in this Agreement shall be deemed to refer to any or all genders or to the neuter gender, as the context may require."

Chapter 2

The Legal Job Interviewer

BEFORE YOU EMBARK ON a legal job interview, you must know something about your adversary—the legal interviewer. I have chosen the word *adversary* quite deliberately; the interviewer is not your friend, no matter how warm or enthusiastic he may be during the interview. His role is not to help you find a job, nor is it really to help his employer find the best possible lawyers. He is a gatekeeper, first and foremost. His job is to examine a host of job applicants clamoring at the gate and let pass only those who, in his judgment, should be given more serious consideration by the organization. As such, he stands between you and your goal—a legal job—and if at any time he perceives a conflict between your goal (landing a job with his employer) and his employer's goal (hiring people who are productive and who fit the employer's image), he will always take the side of his employer.

This is not to say you should treat the interviewer in a hostile or adversarial manner—far from it! It does mean that you should recognize the interviewer for what he is, and be sensitive to his needs, not yours, throughout the interviewing process.

THE INTERVIEWER IS A LAWYER, NOT A PROFESSIONAL INTERVIEWER

In many other professions, you interview first with a human resources executive—a professional interviewer who has been extensively trained in the art of interviewing. Interviewing job candidates is not a peripheral aspect of this individual's job—it is the very heart of his job, and he is an expert at it. This person will use his considerable skills to screen out those people who do not have the requisite skills for the job or who do not fit the organization's style or culture. Only after you pass muster with him will you be allowed (along with others) to interview with the people whose decisions really count—the people in the department or division with whom and for whom you will actually work if you are hired.

By contrast, the legal job interviewing process takes place almost exactly in reverse. Most of the interviews you will go through when seeking a job with a law firm, corporate legal department, or government agency will be with lawyers. Only at the tail end of the interview process (often after you have been made an offer to come on board) will you interview with a human resources or personnel executive, whose function at that point often has been reduced to explaining the compensation and benefits package and showing you where the restrooms are.

If you use the techniques described in most interviewing books to try to impress a legal job interviewer, you are likely not to get very far. Why? Because those interviewing books are written with the professional interviewer in mind. If you find yourself about to interview with a personnel executive or other professional interviewer—such as the legal recruitment coordinator of a law firm—you will need to have the skills to interview with them, too. To that end, you'll find invaluable books on the subject of job interviews listed in the bibliography of this book. These books help you with the two most important aspects of interviewing: being able to provide clear, effective answers to standard interview questions and knowing how to conduct yourself with a professional interviewer.

To succeed in a legal job interview, you must do exactly the opposite of what books on interviewing skills will tell you to do. Some of the keys to success in a legal job interview—which are described in detail in chapter 4—will even seem contrary to common sense, until you apply them in practice and see how well they work.

Lawyers look for different traits in people than managers do and value certain skills higher (and lower) than their counterparts. For example, avoid a sales pitch—anything that smells even remotely of Madison Avenue hype will usually turn a lawyer right off. If you want to sell to a lawyer, your enthusiasm and dynamic presentation skills will not count for much. What will count is your ability to point out to the lawyer the options available to him and assess—in a calm, balanced way—the pros and cons of each option. While you may (and of course should) advocate the course of action you think he should take, you should not push it too hard lest you overlook important facts (which the lawyer knows, but you may not know) that may dictate another course of action. This is, after all, how the lawyer counsels clients!

In short, success in the legal job interview requires that you carry yourself in such a way that you do not appear to be interviewing at all: the lawyer/interviewer will want to have the sort of interaction with you that he knows he will have with you each and every day you are working with him (or for him) on the job. Doing this is not at all easy; some of the specific skills you must master will be discussed at length in chapter 4.

THE INTERVIEWER'S JOB: IT ISN'T WHAT YOU THINK

Having established that your interviewer is not a professional when it comes to interviewing job candidates, what exactly is the lawyer/interviewer's job? If you are like most people before reading this book, you would answer that question in one of the following ways: "to find the best candidate for the job," "to screen out the losers," or "to make sure Firm A enjoys a favorable reputation with XYZ Law School."

Close, but no cigar. You may think this somewhat cynical, but the lawyer/interviewer's primary job is to not do anything that will put him at the other end of the legal job interviewing process. His secondary job is to advance to the next level within his organization. The plain, simple truth is that success as an interviewer will not help a lawyer one whit in staying employed or moving up the legal career ladder. Even if a lawyer were willing to take the time to polish his interviewing skills, he is often too busy to do so. I remember only too well the law firm interviewers who used to come to my law school. After a long day of back-to-back interviews, followed by a lengthy dinner at a fancy restaurant with the most desirable candidates, these poor people would stagger into the law library and work until all hours of the morning just to keep up their billable hours and stay current with their heavy workload.

It should not be too surprising, then, that the lawyer/interviewer is often distracted from the task at hand or views it as being relatively unimportant. More than any other, the fact that the lawyer/interviewer is a lawyer first and an interviewer second often explains the lawyer/interviewer's behavior during a legal job interview. He is often tempted to go by the numbers and pick only those with the most impressive paper credentials, because it requires the least risk, analysis, and time, as the lawyer/interviewer cannot bill anyone for his time spent interviewing job candidates (at least ethically he cannot).

Because the lawyer/interviewer views interviewing as a peripheral aspect of his work only, he knows that an excellent performance will not get him much recognition by his employer. But a poor performance may well make him a laughingstock within his organization. All lawyers wish to avoid the fate of hiring what appeared to be a highly qualified candidate for a midlevel associate's job, only to discover years later that the candidate had falsified all of his credentials (including his admission to the bar!).

Combine this with the lawyer's natural reluctance to take risks, and the result is a cover your rear-end at all costs mentality on the part of the lawyer/interviewer. Simply put, the lawyer/interviewer is most attracted by candidates who will require little selling or explanation within his organization; people whose credentials speak for themselves. That way, if the candidate is hired and fouls something up later on, it is not the lawyer/interviewer's judgment that is at fault, only the candidate's on-the-job performance. If he is hiring an entry-level position, usually filled by recent law school grads, he wants a top grade point average and (if possible) law review membership. For other, higher-up positions, he wants to see lots of experience doing the precise tasks that are called for in the open position, preferably experience at a major, respected firm.

In short, the legal job interviewer is playing a percentage game designed to minimize the risk of error. He will not go out of his way to pursue a candidate who he really likes if the candidate's background or credentials will require explanation or defense within the organization. In dealing with the legal job interviewer, you must take pains to appear to fit as closely as possible to the interviewer's mental picture of an ideal candidate for the job, and be realistic in assessing your paper credentials.

If you are in the bottom quarter of your law school class and are interviewing for your first legal job, your chances of success are better with the small, local law firms in the area where you grew up than in the large, Wall Street law firms. Why? Because your lifelong contacts in the area will help you attract and hold onto clients. Once you have amassed some experience in private practice and have proven your worth as a lawyer (by winning a big case, let's say, or doing something professionally that attracted lots of local media coverage), you can interview with larger firms with greater confidence, knowing that your law school grades will count for less at that point.

THE INTERVIEWER'S GOALS: ENTRY-LEVEL VERSUS CAREER-CHANGE JOBS

Anticipating what the legal job interviewer wants will depend on the interview situation—whether you are interviewing for your first job out of law school (or a summer clerkship between the second and third years of law school) or are looking to change jobs or careers after acquiring some experience in the profession.

Entry-Level Positions

You will probably first encounter the lawyer/interviewer in your second year of law school, as you are seeking that all-important summer clerkship between the second and third years. You will certainly encounter him in your third year if you are looking for a permanent position with a law firm, corporate legal department, or government agency.

What is the interviewer looking for in a law student? The answer will depend on the type of position you are looking for and where the interview is taking place.

The On-Campus/On-Site Approach to Interviewing Law Students

If you are looking for a position in a midsized-to-large law firm in a large metropolitan area, the legal interview may follow the on-campus/on-site process: an on-campus interview with one or more partners and associates of the firm who have flown into town for the sole purpose of interviewing at your law school; followed (if you successfully get past the first screening) by an all-expenses-paid trip to the firm, where you will be interviewed by a battery of people in their offices and taken out to a restaurant for lunch and/or dinner.

The On-Campus Interview. The on-campus interviewers will usually have two traits in common: they are members of their firm's hiring (or legal personnel) committee, and at least one will be a graduate of your law school. Sometimes the interviewers will bring along one of their junior associates who is a recent graduate of your law school so that you can see the sort of person they like to hire generally and so that the interviewers can get the inside story on you from that associate. It is not always easy to tell if their primary objective is to find suitable candidates for first-year associate slots at the firm or to maintain the firm's ties with your law school. Usually it is a little of both.

Sometimes, if you have worked in a particular field or industry before starting law school, you may see the interviewers express some interest in your nonlegal background. This will especially be the case if you worked for one of the firm's corporate clients or in an industry where the firm has special expertise. A firm that specializes in entertainment law with clients in the music industry may, for example, be very interested in hiring a former talent agent. They will not, however, be as interested in someone who spent years pushing buttons in a recording studio, no matter how many autographs he's collected over the years.

Usually, however, the interviewers will be interested only in your performance as a law student. The key word here is *credentials*. Your grade point average must be high. How high will depend on the firm's reputation. Generally, the higher the starting salary for associates, the higher your grade point must be. You should also be involved in law review or a similar publication, and you should have at least some prior connection with the geographic area in which the firm practices. A student from New York City, for example, may have a tough time persuading an interviewer he intends to spend the rest of his life in Kalamazoo, Michigan; conversely, it is my experience that New York City law firms never seem to question an individual's willingness to want to come to New York, no matter where he is from.

Your interest in a specialized field of practice may carry some weight if the firm specializes in that practice, and your performance in that specialty is exceptionally high relative to your overall academic performance. For example, if your passion is international law, a firm specializing in international practice may be quite interested in your membership in your law school's *Journal of Transnational Legal Studies*, your mastery of Mandarin Chinese and Urdu (commonly studied languages like French and Spanish usually don't make the grade here), and the two "books" you earned in international law courses. These focused interests may make up for an otherwise mediocre law school record. If, on the other hand, a candidate who is in the top 10 percent of his class and a member of law review expresses interest in the firm, you will have a difficult time besting him, even if his only other qualification is that he drives a Japanese car.

I am not saying this is fair or even good business on the firm's part. It is simply what happens in an on-campus interview. A candidate whose credentials fall below those of the people the firm has hired in the past is someone who needs to be explained or defended within the firm, and few lawyer/ interviewers are willing to put their career or reputation on the line.

The On-Site Interview.   If your credentials are such that you make it past the on-campus interview, you will usually be invited to spend a day at the firm's offices, where you will interview with a number of partners and associates and will be taken to lunch and/or dinner at a fancy restaurant in town. (Chapter 5 will describe in more detail how you conduct yourself in this situation.)

The individuals with whom you will interview are not selected at random. They are almost always members of the firm's hiring (or legal personnel) committee; sometimes a firm will not put you to a vote until you have been seen by all of the committee's members. Most will be partners, although some associates will usually be thrown in for good measure. If you have expressed interest in a particular area of the firm's practice, you may also interview with one or two partners in that area who are not members of the committee. Finally, you may spend some time talking to an important nonlawyer—the staff person who coordinates the firm's law school recruiting effort. Usually this person or an assistant will walk you from one interview to the next and keep you on your schedule.

What are these lawyer/interviewers looking for? Let's start with the partners. While your credentials are still important at this stage—and you will have to repeat much of the information you doled out at the on-campus interview—what is even more important is your perceived fit with the firm's style, culture, and personnel.

As you walk through the hallowed hallways of Firm A or Corporation B, your interviewers will be looking around and asking themselves, "Does he go with the furniture?" Are they comfortable dealing with you? Do you carry yourself the same way others in the firm do? (Note that this is different from asking if you carry yourself well generally.) Is your image a professional one? Do you appear to be diligent and hardworking? Do you appear to have good judgment? Are you one of us? Do you dress, walk, eat like we do? Will our clients like you?

As you can see, these are extremely subjective questions; no two individuals are likely to come up with precisely the same answer. Moreover, it is not likely that any of your interviewers will ask these questions outright. Indeed, an employer could get into a fair amount of legal trouble if their interviewers did so.

Sometimes, however, it does happen. I recall vividly that once when I was looking for a summer clerkship at my law school, I interviewed with a partner of a prominent firm in a fairly large city in the Deep South. He listened intently to my expression of interest in the firm's work (which was genuine—the firm had a unique specialty that I was interested in at the time), but a quizzical look in his eye told me he wasn't completely convinced. Finally, he leaned over and said in a thick Southern drawl, "Mister Inn-EEE-ko, let me ask you something point blank. Most of our clients here are what you might call hillbilly rednecks—good old boys who have a little too much to drink on a Saturday night, say the wrong things to the wrong people, and get themselves thrown in jail. You've spent your entire life up North. Do you really think you would be comfortable dealing with clients like that?" The real question, of course, which he probably did not think it proper to ask was, "Would our clientele be comfortable baring their souls to someone whose background is so different from theirs?"

Whether a person's cultural fit with an employer is a legitimate criterion for employment is a question much debated in legal circles these days and is beyond the scope of this book. Yet as a general rule, I believe that the farther along you go in interviewing with a particular legal employer, the less important your paper credentials become, and the more important these intangible questions of fitting in become. You must adjust your interviewing style accordingly; whatever you actually say during each on-site interview, you must convince each interviewer that you were born to work for that firm. The fact that your law review case comment is going to be published may well be less important to the interviewer than the fact that you wear plaid sport jackets when the firm look is pinstriped suits.

I have never personally sat in on a legal personnel committee meeting where candidates are being discussed. I have heard, however, and I personally believe that decisions are made more by consensus than by majority vote. In order to succeed in the on-site interview you have to impress favorably almost all of the people who interview you. The one you turn off may well be chairperson of the committee, unbeknownst to you.

Before we leave the on-site interview, a few words about those associates on the committee and the nonlawyer staff person who walks you around from interview to interview. It is very tempting in an on-site interview to save your best performances for the partners you are meeting and relax a bit more when talking to the associates. I believe this is a tragic mistake.

The associates who sit on the firm's legal personnel committee are a special breed; usually they are handpicked by the partners on the committee, who are often among the most powerful partners in the firm. Indeed, it's one of the best ways to identify the up-and-coming associates in a large law firm; some of them may indeed think they are already partners. This tells you right away that their primary loyalty is not to you, the candidate. While they will sit in on the committee meeting that determines whether or not you will be made a job offer—and may well have a vote—you can bet that their favorable opinions of you will not be as important to your future as those of the partners on the committee. They do, however, serve a very important function: to obtain information about you that would not come out in a partner-level interview, where you are probably on your best behavior. Sometimes they will go out of their way to get you to relax and reveal information that will tell the partners you really are not one of them.

Watch out especially if you are taken to lunch by a group of associates with no partners present; being away from the office may tempt you to tell tales out of school. Be assured these associates are smart enough never to do that. Remember Firm A from chapter 1 that took me to lunch at the steak house frequented by movie stars and corporate moguls? There wasn't a partner in the group.

The same rule applies to the nonlawyer who walks you around the office; there is a strong temptation either to talk to him more casually (because he is a nonlawyer) or to open up to him. This latter temptation is especially great, because you're much more likely to let your guard down while walking through the hallways than when sitting in someone's office.

The nonlawyer is quite likely to sit in on the committee's evaluation meeting, and if his view of you is markedly different from the lawyers' view, he will be listened to. In some firms, he may be charged with the task of determining how you will interact with the firm's nonlawyer staff (secretaries, messengers, librarians, and so forth). If he perceives that you are likely to act meanly or improperly toward them, it may be the kiss of death to your candidacy at that firm.

Applying Through Job Postings

Of course, the law firms who choose to follow the on-campus/on-site route tend to be the biggest and most prestigious, with the resources to fly their lawyers around the country interviewing on law school campuses, fly candidates from distant locations to interview at the firm, and pay the candidates' hotel bills. They constitute only a very small percentage of the total number of legal employers, and they certainly have no monopoly on good quality legal work.

Most law students, in fact, will not find their first jobs in this fashion. There will be no on-campus interview. Rather, they will identify one or more geographic locations in which they want to work and focus their attention on firms, companies, etc. in each location. They will send to each firm a copy of their resume and a short cover letter, stating, "I plan to be in your city the week of X and will call you in the next few days to see if you would have some time to meet with me during my stay." They then will schedule a block of interviews in their target location and will usually pay their own airfare and hotel bills or stay with their parents or other relatives.

If you look through the *Martindale-Hubbell Law Directory* and its description of the small-to-medium-sized firms in a particular area, you will note that the majority of lawyers in those firms graduated from law schools in that area. If you are graduating from a law school outside of that area (unless of course it is one of the prestigious, highly visible national law schools), your credentials may have to be as good as if you are interviewing at a large law firm.

What will be more important to a small-to-medium-sized firm are these three factors:

1. The candidate's commitment to work in that geographical location
2. The candidate's commitment to doing the particular type of work that firm does
3. The candidate's potential for keeping the firm's existing clients satisfied and bringing in new clients

This does not mean that questions of fit are irrelevant in the smaller firm environment. Far from it! A small-to-medium-sized law firm is like a family; the partners and associates tend to be more supportive of each other, but there can be a certain tendency to smother, and there will usually be a strong sense of firm identity. Both you and the firm will be extremely unhappy if you are not totally committed to the family business. As one partner of a very small firm once explained to me, "In a place like this it's very important that people see you are on the bus, going the same place that we are. If people have to worry about whether or not you're on the bus, that's going to be a big problem."

Ironically, this is not as much of a concern in the larger law firms, where there is an expectation that many if not most of the young associates hired each year will eventually leave for greener pastures. The question of fit is, however, looked at differently in the smaller firm. In the large firm, the question is does the candidate fit the firm's image or does he look right? In a smaller firm, the question is more likely to be phrased "Does the candidate have what it takes to be a productive member of the family?" or "Is he going to be able to hack it for the long term?"

For a Lateral Hire or a Career Change

First, let's define some key terms. By *lateral hire* I mean a job change made after you have been practicing law for a while and are looking for work in a different legal environment—for example, from a large law firm to a smaller law firm, from a law firm in City A to a law firm in City B, or from a law firm to a corporate legal department or government agency. When you are looking to change the focus of your practice—from a general corporate practice to bankruptcy work, for example—I call it a *career change.*

Obviously, you may be looking to make a lateral move and a career change at the same time. I would argue, however, that changing both your practice and your legal environment at the same time is an extremely difficult move. Once you have started in practice and developed a track record in one or more legal specialties (no matter how short), you tend to become a prisoner of your resume. People looking at your track record will assume that you did something in your life because you enjoyed doing it and that you want to avoid making radical breaks with your past.

Simply put, the longer you stay in the profession, the harder it is to make jagged, radical changes in your career path. You will find, I think, that most people who have made radical changes in their careers have done so only gradually and incrementally. For example, they moved from a larger to a smaller firm first, and then slowly began building up experience in a new and different area of practice as their colleagues gave them overspill work to do in that area.

The candidate must wrestle with his conscience and ask the hard question, "What is it about my current situation that I really detest?" If the answer comes back, "the work I am doing," the candidate will have a much easier time moving into a similar legal environment where he can do the work he enjoys and then, after a couple of years, moving into a different legal environment if he so desires. Similarly, if the answer comes back, "the environment I am in" (for example, the candidate hates working the long hours that are required in a large law firm), he is better advised to change his environment first (in a smaller law firm, for example, the hours are usually more flexible), and then seek work in areas of practice that are more to his liking.

You will most likely find that at this point in your career, your experience will count for more than your academic credentials. You are not likely to be grilled about your grade point average, and you should be slightly insulted if your interviewer asks to see a law school transcript after you have been out of school more than a couple of years. (If you are looking for another position within your first two to three years of practice, your academics may still be important, as you have not had enough time to build up a track record.) Your academic record may, however, help support your argument for a career change. ("I've enjoyed my two years of corporate work, Ms. Jones, but looking back over my academic record I can't help noticing that my best grades were in procedure-related courses and moot courts. I really loved those courses, and my gut tells me that I would be a better fit in litigation.")

One of the questions you are bound to be asked during a job interview will be: "Why do you want to make a change at this point?" We will deal with this question in chapter 7. The important point now is that this question has two possible answers. You must be convinced—and be able to convince your interviewer—either that:

1. You will be a better fit with this new employer than at your current employer, or
2. You are better suited to a type of work *not done* at your current employer or that is *done much better* at your prospective new employer.

The first approach tells the interviewer you are in a lateral situation; the second identifies you as a career changer.

The lawyer/interviewer's concerns with a lateral-hire or career-change candidate will often mirror the candidate's own concerns. When looking at such a candidate, the lawyer/ interviewer wants to know the answers to three questions:

1. Does this candidate have skills and/or contacts that we need here right now?
2. Would this candidate fit in better here than with his current employer?
3. Is this candidate a threat to my job security?

The answer to the first two questions must be yes and to the third, no. Let's look at each of these questions in turn.

Does This Candidate Have Skills and/or Contacts That We Need Here Right Now?

When you are interviewing for a position right out of law school, interviewers usually are not too concerned about your chosen field of practice (although they may ask about your interests). They know that you probably don't have a good idea what you want to do. That's why most of the larger law firms have rotations in the first couple of years, where you are given the opportunity to sample a variety of legal specialties with (sometimes) some choice over your future direction within the firm. In a smaller law firm, of course, these options do not exist: the interviewer will not ask what you want to do, but rather will tell you what the firm does, and you will have to enjoy doing what the firm does because they don't have any choice over their workload themselves.

It is different when you are in the lateral-hiring or career-changing mode. A law firm, corporate legal department, or government agency often does not have the time—and cannot afford—to train people in new areas or fields of practice. If they are in the market for a lateral hire, they usually will want someone who can hit the ground running and begin contributing to the bottom line from his first day of employment. The skills that you have learned with your current employer, the substantive areas of law you have mastered, and the types of transactions you can do in your sleep are the sorts of things the lawyer/interviewer will want to know a great deal about.

In the career-changing situation, rarely will you have all of the skills needed, but you must have at least some carryover skills for which your prospective new employer has an immediate need. As for the rest (the skills you have not yet learned and the transactions you still must master), you must convince the interviewer that you have had at least some exposure to them and have a proven track record as a quick study that will enable you to climb up your learning curve quickly. The interviewer will be asking himself the following questions:

- What sort of experience has the candidate had that makes him think he's better at corporate work than litigation?
- Do we have sufficient corporate work that we can afford to train someone at his level?
- Is the candidate more likely to succeed in corporate work than in litigation?
- Is this candidate sufficiently convinced that corporate practice is his true life's work, or will he change his mind later on and head off somewhere else?

Therefore, the career changer will usually find success only in one of two situations:

1. The employer is willing to train a new employee who has only marginal contact with that area of practice.

2. The employer will insist that the candidate start working in the new area at a reduced salary and at a more junior level than the candidate enjoys at his current employer. For example, if you are a fourth-year associate, the interviewer may say, "We're interested in bringing on more bankruptcy lawyers, but not at your level. If you want to pursue this change in practice, you will have to consider coming on board as a second-year associate."

Would This Candidate Fit in Better Here Than with His Current Employer?

The question of fit is an all-important one in the lateral-hiring situation, both for the candidate and the lawyer/interviewer. After all, the candidate is seeking to do the same sort of work that he is presently doing, so that alone cannot explain the change. The candidate must convince the lawyer/interviewer that he seeks a higher quality practice, a practice located closer to home, a slightly different focus to his practice (e.g., a bankruptcy lawyer who has represented mostly corporations and business entities may want to expand his experience in handling individual bankruptcies), a chance to build his own clientele, practice in a different environment, or some other plausible reason for changing jobs that does not signal a desire to change careers.

Will This Candidate Threaten My Job Security?

By definition, newly minted lawyers fresh out of law school are not threatening to their superiors: they know nothing— and are usually quite aware that they know nothing—about the practice of law and are looking to gain experience and get their feet wet more than they are looking to climb the career ladder. An overwhelming majority of these new lawyers will leave their jobs within the first five years of practice and move on elsewhere, and the senior lawyers within the organization know that.

The same cannot be said of the lateral hire or the career changer, who has some idea of what he wants out of his work and wants to be viewed as a contender for success in his chosen field. The lawyer/interviewer will usually occupy a higher rung on the same ladder the candidate wants to climb and will want to be sure he is not bringing on board the upstart who will knock him off that ladder.

A candidate who convinces the lawyer/interviewer that he has extremely strong skills in his field and a terrific potential for expanding the employer's client base in a dramatic way may be doing himself as much harm as good. After all, the interviewer is the gatekeeper who determines who comes into the organization and who stays out. While his support of a candidate may be subject to some scrutiny by others within the organization, his decision to keep someone out almost certainly will not be questioned ("I just didn't think he would fit in here," "he was much too aggressive," and so forth).

If this sounds unfair to you, you should put yourself for a moment into the interviewer's shoes. If you were worried about being able to hold onto that job over the long term, what thoughts would be going through your mind when interviewing the perfect candidate for a job that could well lead to your position in a couple of years (or a few months)? Would you say to yourself, "His credentials are perfect; I will be doing a great service to my career by sponsoring him and giving him a chance to take over my job in a year or so"? Of course you wouldn't! You would much rather be talking to someone whom you could mentor—someone who knows even less about the field than you do, with a personality that is nonaggressive, self-effacing, and unchallenging.

You may be saying to yourself, "Wait a minute, Mr. Ennico! What you are suggesting is that employers do not seek the best candidates for a position but often are actually looking for mediocrities who won't be a threat to them. How can we compete?" A good question indeed. It all has to do with the American style of management. For example, the Chinese and Japanese get around this, of course, by the rigid seniority system: If you are 30 years old, you simply will never be in a position to challenge the authority of someone in that organization who is 35 or 40 years old. It just isn't done. So the senior executives do not worry as much as their American counterparts about the inadvertent hiring of their replacements.

I do not advocate that we adopt this management system; I merely point out that there is good news and bad news in the American style of management. The good news is that you can indeed unseat someone many years your senior if you have the superior talent, aggressiveness, judgment, and political survival skills to do so. The bad news is that you must not demonstrate in an obvious manner that you have the superior talent, aggressiveness, judgment, and political survival skills to do so.

This is, by the way, what is meant in most organizations by *team playership*. Very often the people who make it to the top in organizations, or who survive the inevitable downsizings and cutbacks, are people who at first blush are not very aggressive. Sometimes they appear to be wimps with little talent, and people will wonder, "How did someone like Charlie ever become vice president?" I suggest to you that these people are in fact quite impressive, because they have learned the difficult lessons of political survival.

Coming on too strong in a legal job interview is one of the cardinal sins that we will discuss at length in chapter 4.

Chapter 3

Before the Legal Job Interview

SUCCESS IN A LEGAL job interview, as in any other professional endeavor, requires preparation and thought. There should be no surprises during the interview itself: you should know what you want, you should anticipate what the lawyer/interviewer wants, you should have ready answers to the standard interview questions, you should have in your mind a list of questions to fill awkward silences, and (most important of all) you should want the job.

No one should ever waste time interviewing for a job they know they will not like; even if they are successful in getting an offer, they will be in a double bind. If they reject the offer, they demonstrate bad faith to the prospective employer, which can only hurt them in the long run (legal employers have long memories, and the legal community, while large, is still small enough that you are certain to encounter some of these people in your practice later on). If they accept the offer, they are committed to a job in which the odds for success are remote and the odds of failure high. Why? Because in the long run, no one can succeed doing work that they don't like doing or being in a job that they know is a dead end for them.

I repeat: you should never walk into an interview situation without knowing in advance that the position, if offered to you, is one you would accept. You will not have this knowledge without doing your homework, sizing up the potential employer, and sizing up the people who are most likely to be your lawyer/interviewers. This chapter discusses the things you should do before you walk into the interview room.

HOW TO SIZE UP THE POTENTIAL EMPLOYER

It is elemental that before interviewing with a particular employer, you must know something about that employer. If the prospective employer is a law firm, you must know the size of the firm, the backgrounds of the key partners, who the key clients are (and how strongly they are attached to the firm), the areas of practice in which the firm specializes, which of these specialties are strong, which are weak, and so forth.

If the prospective employer is a corporation, you must know each of its lines of business, the industry (or industries) in which it competes, the outlook and prospects for each line of business, the financial health of the company as reflected in annual reports and filings with the Securities and Exchange Commission (if its stock is publicly traded), its brands and trademarks, and so forth.

If the prospective employer is a government agency, you must know its mission as set forth in federal or state statutes, the programs which it administers, the tasks lawyers are called upon to play within the agency (in the Department of Justice or a prosecutor's office, it is likely to be litigation, in the Securities and Exchange Commission or a state "blue sky" office, it is likely to be document review), the agency's reputation, and so forth.

The Weaknesses of the Traditional Research Materials

What are the traditional ways of finding out this information? In days gone by, the untutored would (1) look up the employer in the *Martindale-Hubbell Law Directory* or the Aspen Publishers' *Directory of Corporate Counsel*; (2) read the firm resume in his law school's placement office (or obtain a copy from the firm's legal recruitment coordinator), keeping in mind that it is intended as a marketing tool, not an objective statistical description of the firm; (3) if the employer is a corporation, look at the annual report and the latest annual filing with the Securities and Exchange Commission (if the company's stock is publicly traded); and, of course, (4) search for information about the employer on the Internet using your favorite search engine.

While I do not belittle the necessity of doing this type of exhaustive library research (indeed there is a wealth of information in these volumes, if you are thorough and patient), I do feel it necessary to point out some major limitations of this method of preparing for a legal job interview.

First, doing this sort of research takes time, and lawyers and law students have little if any time for nonessential activities. If you are a law student, there are classes to attend, examinations to study for, papers to write, and law review work to be done. If you are a practicing lawyer, there are hours to bill, briefs and memoranda to write, documents to draft, and meetings to attend. I have learned that the more things you plan to do to prepare adequately for a job interview, the less likely you are to do any of them, with predictable results. Indeed, I doubt that most candidates for legal jobs manage to spend more than a few minutes looking at the employer's *Martindale-Hubbell* entry and doing a quick online search before walking into the interview room.

Second, even if you do find the time for careful research, I question the value of the information you are likely to get from the traditional sources. Your research is wasted activity unless it is focused on helping you do two things:

1. Determine whether you would want to work for a particular employer
2. Help you formulate intelligent questions to ask the lawyer/interviewer for that employer

The statistical information you will be able to glean from *Martindale-Hubbell,* the firm resume, or the corporation's annual report is not designed to disclose the inside info you need to be able to deal with these two issues satisfactorily. Few lawyer/interviewers I know are likely to be impressed by your knowing that the firm has 150 lawyers with offices in five states (including Washington, D.C.), specializes in commodities litigation, and just recently won a major case before the United States Supreme Court on the rights of commodities brokers to require arbitration of customer claims. Either they assume you already know this (a lawyer/interviewer will almost never quiz you on your knowledge of the employer's business), or they will think you are trying to show off. In any event, by spouting off this type of information you are not telling them anything that they don't already know. After all, they wrote the firm resume and told *Martindale-Hubbell* what to say about them.

The Two Cardinal Rules of Job Research
In my experience, there are two cardinal rules when researching a potential employer:

1. Gossip or soft information is much more important than statistical or hard information.
2. What you see or hear leaves a more lasting impression in your mind, and is therefore more easily remembered, than what you read or write.

Let's look at each of these rules and see how they apply to researching legal job opportunities.

The Importance of Gossip and How to Get It
Why is gossip so important? Because unfortunately, there is no definitive guide to corporate cultures that can help you

determine what the work environment is like, the rate of employee turnover, the number of reductions in force or downsizings that have occurred over the past couple of years, whether the hours are naturally or artificially long, whether there is an emphasis on a particular ethnic group or practice area within the employer, the extent to which junior lawyers are given responsibility for handling matters and dealing with clients, and so forth.

Sadly, as in many other areas of life, there is a trade-off: obtaining the more intangible or "touchy feely" information about an employer involves accepting a lower standard of reliability than will be the case with hard, statistical information about that employer. This intangible information is subjective; one person's sweatshop is another's paradise, and one person's cutthroat environment is another's dynamic, aggressive culture. More importantly, much intangible information about an employer will tend to come from people who are removed from the employer: former employees whose information may not be up-to-date; people who know the employer only by reputation or by casual contact (for example, the attorney at another firm who has argued or negotiated against attorneys at the firm you want to know about); journalists who have written magazine articles about the employer, often without having any formal training in business or law or experience in the employer's industry; information compiled by trade associations or journals; and the like.

The best and most reliable source of intangible information about an employer is, of course, people like yourself who work there in the position for which you are interviewing. These sources must be handled with care, and the information they provide weighted to account for their position within the organization. A senior associate at a large law firm who is up for partnership this year, for example, is walking on eggshells and is not likely to say anything bad about his employer for fear it will get back to the powers on the legal personnel committee. A first-year associate at the same firm may not be as committed to the firm but also does not have the experience to see the big picture. Because you do not know who talks to whom within the employer, you would not want to ask any question you would not ask an interviewer from that employer; this will further reduce the value of the information you obtain.

This is not to say that you should not contact people at the target employer (although of course you should do so as discreetly as possible), only that you will seldom be able to get the best information out of them in a way that will not increase the risk of your being screened out of the interview process. For the same reason that I never read a biography of a politician who is still in office (he's not about to write about the good stuff because he still needs to remain on good terms with a lot of people), but only a politician who has retired (and is therefore free to tell all within the limits of the libel laws), I believe that the best source of intangible information about an employer (although certainly not the most unbiased) is someone who has recently left that employer under generally favorable conditions.

Don't Read; Watch and Listen
The second cardinal rule of researching a potential employer is that what you see or hear leaves a more lasting impression in your mind, and therefore is more easily remembered,

than what you read or write. I do not have a background in cognitive psychology, but I find I have an easier time remembering stories and cases that were particularly vivid or funny than I do law review articles, hornbook chapters, or legal outlines. I believe the same is true in researching a potential employer.

Once I was looking at a career opportunity at a smaller law firm—let's call it Firm Y. I met with Firm Y's name partner and found him to be an awfully sweet and likable person. Some of the other attorneys looked a bit haggard around the edges, but I attributed this to the nature of the practice. Several days later I met with another lawyer in the same community, who without any prodding from me volunteered that Firm Y was a notorious sweatshop whose name partner "while he always comes across as a sweet and likable person, has a reputation for taking you for everything you're worth once your foot is in the door. Unless you get an employment agreement in writing with him, you'll end up working 90 hours a week for a salary that won't even pay your rent." Without suggesting that I was talking to Firm Y, I called up three other lawyers in the same community, all of whom confirmed Firm Y's reputation as a sweatshop and the name partner's trickiness in dealing with new hires. While this of course was only circumstantial evidence, there is an old saying: "If one person calls me a horse, I laugh; if three people call me a horse, I go out and buy a saddle." I did not pursue the opportunity at Firm Y any further.

So How SHOULD You Research an Employer?

How should you research a potential employer? Keeping in mind the two cardinal rules of researching a potential employer, I would suggest that you focus first on magazine and journal articles about the employer, and then try to network through to someone who can give you the inside information you really need, either in person or over the telephone. Moreover, you should spend about 25 percent of your available research time on the first task, and 75 percent on the second. A good personal contact will always be 10 times more useful than a written source.

Use the Internet Strategically!
The Internet is both a blessing and a curse when it comes to researching law firms, corporations, and other legal employers. The blessing, of course, is the time it saves you when doing employer research: in just a few clicks of a mouse, you can find a law firm's website, blogs from some of the firm's partners, and articles written about the firm in the major news media.

The curse is that the information you want to find out about an employer won't be available on the firm's website or any official blogs or sites relating to the firm. Those sites have been sanitized to the point where they are pretty much useless to the job searcher (except they are usually pretty good at posting up-to-date biographical information about the employer's partners or executives).

What you are looking for is the inside scoop—what they're doing wrong, why people might be unhappy working there, which partners are leaving for other firms and taking their practices with them, whether people are rushing to join the firm or bailing like rats leaving a sinking ship. And that information is tough to find, because the people posting that information on the Web are doing their best to avoid being picked up on the employer's radar screen. Even when you find something on a law firm or other employer, you have to take it with a ton of Morton's finest. People who post negative information on blogs usually have an axe to grind, and you cannot count on them to be entirely objective. Quite a few bloggers have more than a screw or two loose, to put it bluntly, and you will have to do some judicious reading between the lines to figure out if a Web posting is truly newsworthy or is to be written off as opinionated blather.

Having said that, there are a few websites that can be counted on for reliable (and generally accurate) information about legal employers that goes beyond the firms' press releases, among them:

- *www.abovethelaw.com*
- *www.judged.com*
- *www.law.com* (the website of the *National Law Journal*)
- *www.americanlawyer.com* (the website of *The American Lawyer*)
- *www.lawjobs.com*
- *www.findlaw.com*

Also, keep in mind that the information you find on the Internet, aside from the possibility of it being merely useless, can be really, *really* old. In these days of instant information and communication via the Internet, any text-based data becomes out of date in a real hurry. I've seen entries on Wikipedia about law firms that are broken up—the former associates are probably too busy looking for jobs to update the firm's Wikipedia entry! Keep an eye on when the information was posted to a blog or when a site was last updated.

Magazine Articles: The More Gossip, The Better
You should begin with articles about the employer that have appeared in business magazines and trade journals. You can look these up in the *Reader's Guide to Periodical Literature* and the *Index to Business Periodicals* available at any library.

With respect to law firms, which often are not written about in the business press, you should go to a law library (usually there will be one in or near your county courthouse or at a local law school that will give nonstudents limited access). Look up the employer's name in the index to the *National Law Journal, The American Lawyer*, or any other regional or local publication that focuses on the legal profession, not developments in the law itself (a state bar journal or the American Bar Association's magazines, for example, will not have the type of information you need).

When reading magazine articles, especially those in general business magazines such as *Fortune, Forbes*, and *Business Week*, try to stay clear of articles on a specific new development (for example, the employer's introduction of a new product or the appointment of a new chief executive officer). Try instead to find articles describing general trends in the employer's industry, business lines, or financial condition. Usually you can tell from the headline, which is usually reprinted in the standard indexes, whether the article is specific or general in nature.

Keep in mind that magazine articles are fine, but they represent the view of an outsider looking in, not an insider (as you want to be) looking out. Reporters after all are only as good as their sources, and lawyers are notoriously reticent to tell outsiders what really goes on at their shops (something to do with preserving client confidentiality and all that). Moreover, journalists value their sources and usually will not divulge information if the risk of losing a valued source outweighs the newsworthiness of the information.

Generally, given the choice, I play down articles in general business magazines (and their websites) and focus my attention instead on articles in industry trade journals. While these are subject to some of the same restrictions as general business magazines (the need to avoid offending sources, for example), they tend to be written by people who are more experienced with the industry and the key players in that industry and so tend to ask the right questions more frequently. If you are lucky enough that your prospective employer is in an industry with a highly respected newsletter that also publishes industry gossip (such as *Asset Securitization Report*, a biweekly publication that reports on developments in the structured finance industry on Wall Street), you should know what that newsletter has written about your target employer. You may even want to call one of the editors for some behind-the-scenes information. If the publication is small enough, the editors may be extremely flattered that you thought enough of them to call and will usually be cooperative if they think you will eventually become a subscriber—or better yet, a source of industry information once you find employment.

How to Read the Employer's Own Literature
While magazine and trade journal articles are good sources of the right information about an employer, they are only the

starting points of your research. If you are interviewing with a law firm or corporation, you should at least glance at the firm resume or the corporation's annual report, but not for any hard, statistical information that may be printed there. Look instead for clues to the organization's structure and future plans.

In an annual report, for example, I would read the president's message to shareholders. How optimistic or pessimistic is senior management about the company's future? Which lines of business have performed, and which have not? (You don't want to be hired by a poorly performing unit—they are the first to downsize.) You should read also the brief descriptions of the corporation's business lines. Which are the core businesses, and which lie at the periphery? (The latter will be the first to be sold off or shut down.) In the corporation's proxy statement and annual report to the Securities and Exchange Commission, read the biographies of senior management. Which functional disciplines (such as marketing or finance) or business groups did they come from? Is there one unit or discipline that has contributed a disproportionately large share of senior managers? If so, that's where you want to be.

In a firm resume, don't read about the lawyers; read instead about the *clients*. Who are they, how healthy are they, and how long have they been clients? Is the firm overly dependent on a single client? If so, how strong is the firm's attachment to that client? Are firm partners on the client's board of directors, for example? If you are looking at a firm that is heavily dependent on one client for its business, you should research the client as if you were seeking employment there (for you are, in a way). As that client goes, so goes the firm. If the firm has many clients, is that because they are specialists in a particular area of practice? Patent and trademark firms will usually list many clients, but may not do anything for those clients outside the intellectual property field. Similarly, investment banking clients normally spread their work among many law firms depending on their specialties—Firm M will do the investment bank's real estate transactions, Firm N will do the public offerings, while Firm P will do the maritime and admiralty work. If you sense that the firm's reputation rests on a particular specialty, you had better want to specialize in that area of practice. Any specialty that is heavily dependent upon tax benefits from the federal or state governments should be scrutinized especially closely, as such a specialty can disappear overnight if there is a change in the tax laws.

Talk to People Who Know the Employer from the Inside Out

Your best information about a prospective employer will not come from the written word but rather from people. It is never too early or too late to begin building up a personal network of contacts who can be sources of information not available to the general public. After all, this is where reporters and other journalists get their scoops: why not you? Let's say you are interested in Firm X; how do you go about finding out what really goes on there? Who ya gonna call?

Alumni. First, you should visit or call your law school's placement office, even if it has been some time since you graduated. They will usually have their alumni listed on a computerized database and can (for a small charge or for free) give you the names, addresses, and telephone numbers of any law school alumni who work at Firm X and other similar firms in the same city. You probably have already figured out that your college placement office can furnish you with similar information about graduates of that college.

If there are no alumni working at Firm X, what about one of Firm X's key clients? If you really want to see someone at a law firm jump to attention, call and indicate to his secretary that an executive of one of his important clients suggested you call.

If there are no alumni working at Firm X or one of Firm X's clients, how about one of Firm X's rival firms in that city? (I would define a *rival firm* as a firm of comparable size, doing the same sort of work for the same sort of clientele.) Who knows? If you succeed in impressing a lawyer at a rival firm, the latter may think to himself, "Gee, why should Firm X get all the hot prospects?" And you may find yourself interviewing at the rival firm!

Bar Association Contacts. Take a look at Martindale-Hubbell and see if there is a local or regional bar association in which most of Firm X's lawyers participate. If there is (and there usually will be), call the bar association, find out which committees are most likely to have lawyers from Firm X in your desired area of specialty (for example, if you are interested in representing banks, you will probably want to talk to lawyers on the business/commercial law committee), and then find out if there are any college or law school alumni participating in those committees.

Friends and Relatives. Personal contacts are great. Talk to friends, relatives of friends, friends of your relatives— anyone who may have inside knowledge of Firm X. You can also try contacts at one of Firm X's clients or at one of its rivals.

Legal Recruiters or Headhunters.   You should find out which legal recruiters—or headhunters as they are commonly known—work in the city where Firm X is located, and ask them about Firm X's reputation in the marketplace. You will be surprised how much these people know; lawyers at firms throughout the city are daily telling them their tales of joy or woe. You will also be surprised how much the recruiters will tell you; since lawyers change jobs fairly frequently these days, you are a potential source of business to them. They may even be able to introduce you to someone who just recently left Firm X for greener pastures, who will be only too willing to tell you more than you ever wanted to know about Firm X and how they treat their people. (You should keep in mind, of course, that such a person is not likely to be very objective about Firm X, especially if he left under less-than-ideal circumstances.) You are not asking the recruiters to help you find a job at Firm X; you are merely asking for help in networking through to someone who can answer some specific questions about Firm X and its practice and reputation in the legal community.

Other Job Candidates.   Finally, you should ask others who are looking for jobs in the same area what they have heard about Firm X. Of course, these people have no incentive to help you in your networking; they may even view you as a competitor and steer you away from opportunities that they may be pursuing. Nonetheless, I think it is worth a try, especially if you latch onto someone who is willing to swap information about Firm X for information about an employer you have researched in which he is interested.

When You Find a Good Contact, What Do You Say?

What should you say when asking a total stranger about Firm X? You should be very careful what you say, because you don't know this person, and if you don't know a person, you don't know who that person knows. This person you are talking to may be the golfing buddy of the chairperson of the legal hiring committee at Firm X!

First, you should identify yourself and the reason for your call. Most people will take the time to be helpful, but only if you are straightforward with them. You should say, "This will only take 5 (or 10) minutes," and then stick to your deadline unless the other person takes you over the limit. You should say that you are merely looking to learn something about Firm X and its local reputation and that you are not calling with any ulterior motive (such as obtaining a job at the contact's employer).

Second, show that you know something about the target employer and its practice or business, so as to discourage the contact from merely reciting the party line. If the contact is not very helpful, ask (in a polite and nice way) if he would be willing to introduce you to someone else in his organization who has had more direct contact with your target employer than perhaps he has had. You could suggest that perhaps there is someone in his organization who has worked at Firm X in the past or has recently negotiated a transaction on the other side of Firm X's attorneys.

Be sure to express vigorously your thanks for any scrap of information he may deign to throw you, and follow up with a thank-you letter even if he has not been very helpful. Once you have found employment, be sure to send him your business card and a short note letting him know how he helped you sort out your thinking.

Networking as a Way of Life

Networking is probably the most productive way to obtain (legally) nonpublic information about any person or organization you are interested in contacting for any reason. But keep in mind that the shoe may be on the other foot someday. Your contact may be calling you for assistance, and you will be obligated to do whatever you can.

Also, keep in mind that even if your networking proves to be unproductive, whether you know it or not you are polishing your interviewing skills with these faceless contacts in a nonthreatening way. Nothing is at stake, and the worst they can do is hang up on you (few will). Even if you do not get what you want out of them, they will be flattered that you called, and if you stay in touch with them, you may find there will come a time in your career when they are in the best possible position to help you.

One final rule of networking etiquette: while you should use the information you have obtained through networking in the job interview to show your enthusiasm for the position and the thoroughness of your research, *you must never disclose the name of the person who furnished you with that information.*

Attorneys are known for their discretion. While the lawyer/interviewer may be dying to know how you found out about the firm's growing municipal bond practice in state X and close ties to gubernatorial candidate Smith, you must protect your sources like a good investigative reporter. A good way to handle this is to say something like, "Well, good news gets around fast," and then follow up with a question of your own to get off the subject.

HOW TO SIZE UP THE INTERVIEWER

Finding out what the target employer is really like and obtaining nonpublic information that you can use to your advantage during the job interview itself is only half the battle. To be truly successful in a legal job interview and stand out from the crowd of people competing against you, it is necessary to know something about your lawyer/interviewer(s) before you walk in the door.

Step # 1: Know "Who's Who in the Zoo"

The first stop is your law school placement office. By obtaining a copy of the firm resume or corporate materials that are on file there, you will be able to tell at a glance who the members of the firm's legal personnel committee are, the names of the other attorneys in the corporation's legal department (and, more importantly, who reports to whom within the organization), and the division heads of the legal staff of the government agency.

Not all lawyers employed by an organization will be lawyer/interviewers. Only a very select handful will be chosen to perform this task, and your first task must be to identify the subset of lawyer/interviewers that lurks within the larger pool of attorneys employed by the target organization.

Lawyer/interviewers will generally fall into one of two categories: either they are members of a legal personnel committee or other select group of lawyers to whom the organization delegates the delicate task of screening candidates for employment, or they are lawyers to whom you will directly report if you are hired at the target organization.

Finding out the names of the lawyers to whom you would report if you are hired is relatively simple. Usually the job description will contain this information, as in the case of a newspaper ad that says "reports to the assistant general counsel in charge of patents and trademarks." In the case of a lateral hire or career change, however, this information may not be as easily obtained. In these cases you will have to call the target employer's personnel office and find out verbally who heads up the division's legal staff or who the senior partners in the firm's bankruptcy department are. Sometimes you will not be able to find out this all-important information until the initial interview; in this case one of your first questions for the lawyer/interviewer should be: "How is the department structured, and who reports to whom within the department?"

If you are interviewing for your first legal job out of law school, virtually all of your interviews will be with members of the legal personnel committee. Finding out who these people are should be as easy as looking at the firm resume on file in your law school placement office. If this information is not available, the placement office personnel should be able to get it for you (and for your competition) without much difficulty, or you may wish to call the firm's recruitment coordinator and obtain the information directly. There is a risk, of course, in taking the latter course, since if you identify yourself to the recruitment coordinator, he may be tempted to tell a member of the committee to "be careful when talking to so-and-so from Law School X; he's been calling here asking all kinds of questions." As in so many other aspects of the information gathering process, your ability to be discreet counts for much here. One way to do this is to call the firm, ask for the recruitment coordinator's secretary (not the coordinator himself), and without identifying yourself, say that you are interested in writing a letter to the chairman of the legal personnel committee and want to know the correct spelling of his name. At least you will know one name through this method. Another way of achieving your goal is to make friends with a librarian at another law firm in the same city. It is my experience that law librarians all know one another, and if he likes you he may be willing to place a discreet telephone call to his counterpart at the target firm and ask for a list of the legal personnel committee members.

Step # 2: Learn about Individual Interviewers

Once you have found the names of the legal personnel committee members and the most influential partners in the department or division in which you will be working if hired, your task is a simple one: find out as much about each one of them as you possibly can before you walk into his office. As will be seen, this is a process that continues right up to the moment (and sometimes after) the interview begins.

His Curriculum Vitae

The first stop, of course, is *Martindale-Hubbell*. There you will find the individual's date of birth, educational history (where he graduated from college and law school and years of graduation), a list of publications and bar memberships, professional honors and awards, and (sometimes) area of practice concentration. If you are looking at a corporate legal department or government agency, the Aspen Publishers' *Directory of Corporate Counsel* may be a better place to start, as more corporations list detailed information about their legal staff there than they do in *Martindale-Hubbell.*

Common Interests in the Law

If you find that the lawyer/interviewer you are research- ing has written a number of articles for law reviews or bar journals, should you read any or all of them prior to the interview?

My advice is usually no. It takes up too much time, you probably won't remember much of importance (and will risk misquoting the article when actually speaking to the lawyer/interviewer), and you will appear to be brownnos- ing (or worse, stalking) if you show any detailed familiarity with the interviewer's written work. You should, however, know the titles of the articles he has written, and if you have the time you should read the brief synopsis or execu- tive summary that usually appears at the beginning of each article. This will give you an idea of the particular issues or problems in which the interviewer is interested, and if you can (sincerely and genuinely) make the connection between the interviewer's interest and something you your- self have written about or studied, so much the better. The key words here are *genuinely* and *sincerely*. If the lawyer/ interviewer thinks you are coming across as too polished or are trying to brownnose him, he may be tempted to turn the tables on you by asking a series of detailed (and embarrassing) questions to find out just how closely you have followed his work.

What are you looking for, then, in studying the interviewer's biography? You are looking for something in common— if the interviewer is a graduate of your college or law school or has written extensively in an area you are currently writing about.

Make sure you have something to talk about that will set you apart from the competition. Rarely will *Martindale-Hubbell* and the other legal directories give you all of the information you will need to know in a legal job interview.

The Really Good Stuff

To get the really good stuff about a lawyer/interviewer, you must resort to networking and gossip, just as you did when researching the target employer. Talking to other attorneys in the community can be very useful here if you are in a lateral-hiring or career-changing situation. While professionals are notoriously uneasy about tattling on their colleagues in the bar, most will give you a balanced presentation of the scuttlebutt if they feel they can trust you to be discreet. Keep in mind that you are not trying to find out about the lawyer/ interviewer's sex life or personal idiosyncrasies, the sort of things people are naturally reluctant to talk about. You are trying to find out harmless things: his hobbies, number of children, political or community interests, professional interests (bar association committees and the like), significant cases or business transactions he is known for, client contacts, and so forth. When you have learned something about an interviewer that might help you establish rapport with him, write down a question that you think will help open him up on an area of mutual interest or concern and get him talking away about something the two of you find fascinating.

Study the Interviewer's Office

Finally, keep your eyes open when you walk into the interview room (or the interviewer's office). If you arrive for the interview early and (lucky you!) are asked to wait in the office for a couple of minutes as the interviewer has been detained in a meeting, look around you and drink in every detail. Are there paintings of sailboats on the wall? What sorts of legal and nonlegal books are on the bookshelf? If there are bound volumes or Lucite awards anywhere in the office, what types of transactions or cases were they and how much money was at stake? Are there any memorabilia or toys on the interviewer's desk? What does the furniture look like—contemporary (metal and glass), traditional (solid hardwoods), or beat up (passed on from partner to partner over the generations)?

Look at the inevitable pictures of the interviewer's family—are the children holding any objects (like a baseball glove) that may offer clues to their parent's hobbies or interests? Do the family pictures face the interviewer, or is his back turned to them? Is the interviewer's desk tidy or disorganized? Is there a wall of paper separating you from the interviewer, or is everything off to one side? Does the interviewer's desk face toward the window or the door?

Little details like these can speak volumes about a person, and you should be attentive to them every minute you are interviewing. Even when you have not been given an opportunity to size up the interviewer's desk and office before the interview, you should take advantage of every moment during the interview to do so. By using the techniques described in chapter 4, you will have plenty of time to make the necessary assessments. By using common sense, you can usually determine from the arrangement of a person's office or desk how compulsive he is, how important his family life is to him, what he does with his spare time, and the type of work that means the most to him.

Two things you should never do when in an interviewer's office: open up any of his desk drawers, or go behind his desk to look at something at closer range. The former is an invasion of privacy; the latter is viewed by most people as an invasion of the interviewer's personal space which he may well resent.

The Interviewer's Appearance

Finally, when you greet the interviewer, make a detailed note of his appearance. How well (and how conservatively) does he dress? Is his presentation formal or informal? Does he ramble on or watch every word? How does he use his space—does he keep the desk between you and him or do the two of you sit on the same side of the desk? Does he make regular eye contact or is he looking through you?

You should keep in mind that employers pick their lawyer/ interviewers because they are exemplars of what the employer wants in its lawyers. Indeed, one of the surest ways to spot the up-and-coming lawyers in an organization is to see which ones are named to the legal personnel committee. Ask yourself constantly during the interview, "Do I want to be like him someday?" That is the question your prospective employer wants you to ask. If the answer is no, you need try to impress the interviewer no further.

CLEAN UP YOUR ACT ON THE INTERNET

The Internet has created a culture of self-expression unparalleled in human history. At no other time in history have people around the world felt so free to make public the intimate details of their lives, their thoughts, their feelings, their political views, their preferences (sexual, culinary, and otherwise), and so forth. While the Internet is a terrific tool that can help you research potential employers, it is also a terrific tool to help the employers research you. And rest assured they will. So before you start going on interviews, get online and clean up your act.

If you receive an offer to interview at any decent-sized law firm, be assured the firm's recruiting personnel will be checking the Internet looking for information about you— your background, interests, personality, and, ahem, short-comings. Remember that the lawyer/interviewer's primary goal is to find ways to screen you out, and the Internet has cost many a fine job applicant their chance at a future in the law.

If the firm's personnel isn't checking you out on the Internet, be assured that the junior personnel of the firm— especially associates at large law firms—will be combing through YouTube looking for videos of your college fraternity toga party or a blog posting about you from one of your ex-girlfriends or ex-boyfriends. Because if they uncover any dirt and share it with their superiors, they will come across looking awfully good and may actually get a bonus for helping the firm avoid a costly hiring mistake.

If you are planning a career in the legal profession, now is the time to clean up your act online. Search your name and do your best to remove any embarrassing or inappropriate postings. Concentrate especially on locating (and removing, if need be) information or images about the following:

- Your personal life, hobbies, or sexual history
- Your participation in illegal (like smoking marijuana), immoral (you need an example?), or simply inappropriate activities
- Your opinions on subjects that people tend to have strong opinions on, such as religion, sexual preference, or politics—no matter what they are, they are sure to offend at least one person you interview with

My rule of thumb here is if it's something you wouldn't want your worst enemy getting their hands on, get it the hell off the Internet! Like it or not, succeeding as a lawyer will require you to keep your personal life, opinions, and preferences close to the vest (quite literally), and it's best to get into the habit now. Exhibitionism is for movie stars, recording artists, professional athletes, and celebrities, not the anonymous grinds who toil in America's legal industry.

Chapter 4

Conducting Yourself
in a Legal Job Interview

YOU HAVE NOW PASSED the preliminary hurdles in the legal job interviewing process. You have researched the employer and the interviewers, you have a long list of questions that you have carefully memorized, and you have done something that has made the employer want to interview you for a position (such as answering an advertisement, contacting a headhunter, or signing up in your law school placement office). You are now on your way to the interviewer's office or one of the airless cubicles in your law school placement office (why is it that so many placement offices are located in the law school basement?), where the interview is going to take place.

How should you conduct yourself during the interview? What should you do with your hands? Your feet? Should you look the interviewer in the eye or at a point three inches above his head? How much talking should you do? How much talking should the interviewer do? What is the best way to close the interview? Do you have to send a thank-you note afterward?

To combine all of these questions in a single question: how do you put your best foot forward and maximize the chances of making a positive impression on this fellow human being whom fate has thrown into the same room with you for a few brief but precious minutes? This chapter helps you answer this most important of all interviewing questions.

Before we begin our dissection of the legal job interview, it may be wise to take a quick and humorous look at how NOT to interview for a legal position. A friend of mine tells this story, and it is one of my personal favorites:

> I wasn't one of the brightest in my law school class, but I wasn't one of the dumbest either. I was interviewing for a summer clerkship with a large law firm, so of course I knew I was up against some tough competition. Some of those guys can be pretty condescending too, especially if your law school isn't Harvard or Yale. But I never knew the meaning of condescension until I interviewed one day with a lawyer from a prominent firm from a medium-sized city in the Midwest. (To avoid any libel of an otherwise excellent firm and a very livable city, I am calling it "Midwest City.")
>
> I had signed up to interview with the Midwest City firm out of curiosity more than anything else. It was

the only Midwest City firm that interviewed at my law school that year, I had some distant relatives who lived in Midwest City, and frankly I was dating someone who was originally from that area. I just wanted to find out if firms in the Midwest were any more laid-back than firms in the Northeast, with the thought that if I liked these guys enough I might be willing to split my summer. I noted that I was one of only three people who had signed up to interview for the firm, none of them law review or top 10 percent, so I thought my chances for a callback were pretty good.

The interviewer from the Midwest City firm was one of the senior partners: a tougher-looking person I have never seen before or since. He glared at me when I walked into the interview room, perused my resume briefly, let it drop to the floor, and then sat back, crossed his arms, and began to interrogate me with some of the most pointed, offensive questions I have ever been asked in an interview setting. If my grades were so good in college, how come I didn't go to Harvard? Why had I done so poorly in Contracts first semester? Why wasn't I a member of the Order of the Coif (a national honor society for law students; to be a member one must be in the top 10 percent of one's class)? Why hadn't I been selected for law review? Why wasn't I looking at less prestigious firms, since it was clear I didn't have what it took to be seriously considered by a firm like his? Why was I talking to a firm from Midwest City when it was clear I hadn't any prior connection to the city?

After a few minutes I began to get angry. I held back at first, because I thought this was the adversary interview that all of the books on interviewing talk about, and I wanted to demonstrate that I was tough and could defend a difficult case. (This particular partner, I found out later, was one of the top trial lawyers at his firm and so was probably pretty accustomed to cross-examination.) Perhaps he was trying to test me to see if I could handle a difficult situation.

But with each passing minute it became more and more clear that he was not playing an interviewing game with me. He was sincerely offended that someone with my less-than-stellar credentials had applied to interview with his firm; he quite clearly believed that someone like me should not even be considering a career in law; and he wanted to do everything in his power to put me down and punish me for my boldness. In short, the guy was a total jerk. Finally, after what seemed like a hailstorm of fire and brimstone in the form of one negative question after another, he interrupted my answer in midstream, threw his notepad down on the floor (he had not taken a single note that I saw), folded his arms, turned away from me, and said, "Okay, I've heard all I need to know. Now, what do you want to know about the firm?"

At this point I was too mad to speak. I was as close to physically assaulting someone as I ever hope to get in my life. I decided that I wasn't going to blow up and give him the satisfaction of knowing that his judgment about me was correct. Knowing that nothing I could do would interest him in me (and having decided that I wouldn't work in his firm if they paid the highest starting salary in the United States), I calmly pulled out a small notepad and pen from my jacket pocket, poised myself to jot down notes, and asked the partner, "Tell me, Mr. So-and-So,

I see from *Martindale-Hubbell* that you went to Harvard Law School. Tell me, what was your rank in class?"

The partner almost fell out of his chair. He turned to face me, stunned, and asked in bold disbelief, "Why is that of any importance to you?" I said, "Well, to be honest, yours is the first firm outside the Northeast I've interviewed with. I'm looking primarily at firms in the Northeast, because everyone knows the quality of practice there is so much better than it is anywhere else, if not necessarily the quality of life. I'm curious to find out how much of a trade-off in quality in practice I'll have to make if I settle for your firm." The partner began to turn red and sputtered, "I'll have you know, I was in the top quarter of my class at Harvard." "Thank you," I said, and jotted the information down on my pad, asking as I wrote, "And were you a member of the *Harvard Law Review?*" His eyes widened as if I had pulled a knife on him. "No, I wasn't, but I was editor of one of the other journals there. You could have known that had you read *Martindale-Hubbell.*" "I know, sir, but then I also knew that you were not Order of the Coif so you could not have been in the top 10 percent of your class either," I said.

"Now tell me," I continued, "did you go directly to your present law firm? Or was there a stop in between? Did you start somewhere else?" The partner couldn't believe his ears. He was clearly amazed, but instead he sat back in his chair, squirming at the taste of his own medicine, and said, "No. I went directly to this firm." "Did you look at law firms elsewhere?" "No, I didn't." "Why didn't you? You're not a native of Midwest City, and you didn't go to college here." (I knew this from *Martindale-Hubbell*). "I don't think I have to answer that."

Now I had him. I threw my notepad down on the floor, directly on top of his, took off my glasses very slowly, looked him straight in the eye, and said, "Mr. So-and-So, there's a lot here that just does not fit. If you were in the top quarter of your class at Harvard, a journal editor to boot, you could have gone anywhere in the country to practice law. What the devil are you doing in Midwest City?" The partner turned beet red, and his hands started clutching the armrests on his chair as if he were holding himself back. I sat back in my chair and said, "I don't see any point in continuing this discussion. You see, I care as much as you do about working with quality lawyers. And in treating me the way you have in the past few minutes you have just turned off the best summer clerk you are ever going to get from this law school this year. Because only three students signed up to interview with your firm, and I'm the best of them. Anybody who's better—in your definition of better— wouldn't be caught dead talking to a firm from Midwest City when they know they can work for a firm from New York, or Washington, D.C., or San Francisco. I can think of only two reasons that might explain your decision to practice law in Midwest City: either you were dating someone from there, which as it so happens I am right now, or you just couldn't get into anyplace better. Next time, before you tear into someone, try to remember that beggars can't be choosers."

I didn't give him the chance to respond. By this point he was furious, quaking with anger, and was trying to keep from becoming physically violent, much as I had earlier in the interview. I picked up my pad, turned my back on this loser, and stormed out.

I didn't have too much of a chance to gloat about my "turnabout is fair play" treatment of the interviewer, though. For there, waiting to interview with that same monster, was one of my best friends in law school, who happened to hail from Midwest City. This interview obviously meant a great deal to him, and I felt lousy the rest of the day knowing that I had set him up for one of the worst experiences of his life (although, frankly, I don't have any assurance that the interviewer would have treated him any differently). When I saw my friend later that evening, he said, "What did you say to that guy? I couldn't get a word out of him the first couple of minutes. I thought he was going to have a stroke!"

I am sure many of you had a twinge of satisfaction in reading my friend's account of a particularly nasty interview. There are two morals, however, to this story, neither of them favorable to my friend. While many lawyers are fine examples of humanity, the legal profession like any other has its share of jerks. Learning to survive in a legal job environment means learning to deal with all kinds of personality types, egos, and political styles. Later on in this chapter we will discuss dealing with the difficult interviewer.

What is more important, though, is the effect that my friend's conduct had on the entire interviewing process. By his own admission, he hurt one of his best friends in law school without intending to. Even more serious, he may have poisoned his law school's reputation with that law firm; if I were that interviewer, with the titanic ego he had, I would have recommended to my legal personnel committee that we write that law school off for good. If the law school's placement director (or dean) heard about my friend's conduct from the interviewer or from other alumni who were working at that firm, I think my friend's reputation would have been in jeopardy, and he may have been cut out of the interviewing program (these sorts of things routinely happen, although they did not happen to my friend).

One thing I have learned in my years of practicing law: no matter how large the profession may seem (just look at the size of those *Martindale-Hubbell* volumes, after all), you are constantly bumping into people you've worked with, people you've interviewed with, people you went to law school with, people you negotiated or litigated against, over and over again. You cannot afford to alienate anyone you encounter in your practice, even if it makes you feel good at the time. Perhaps this explains why some of the most successful lawyers alive today have the blandest and most colorless of personalities: they don't light any fires, but they don't create any negative impressions either! With that in mind, let's begin our discussion of the legal job interview.

YOUR MIND-SET AS YOU WALK IN THE DOOR

It is so easy to blow an important interview before it is even started. Too many job candidates are so eager to get down to business that they forget an interview is as much a social occasion as a business one. Your first task, and perhaps your only task, is to get the interviewer to like you as a person.

If a person likes you, he is usually willing to overlook an occasional slight or faux pas and is more likely to give you the benefit of the doubt in chancy situations. As the social psychologists tell us, likes usually are attracted to likes (or more precisely, people are attracted to other people whom they perceive to be like themselves, regardless of the actual truth), and people are more likely to think good things about (and do good things for) people whom they find attractive. This is not limited to physical attractiveness, although being considered extremely attractive in the physical sense cannot hurt your chances of winning an interviewer over.

Most books on interviewing stress the importance of making a good first impression when you walk in the interviewer's door, and give a few basic, commonsense rules for beginning a job interview:

- Relax!
- Don't appear to be worried or under pressure to get a job quickly—never let them see you sweat.
- Don't appear to be overly eager or artificially enthusiastic. Be pleasant but not to the point where you might appear to be obsequious or smarmy.
- Greet the interviewer with a smile and a firm (but not bone-crushing) handshake.

This is all well and good, but when you are interviewing for a job you really want, and when there is much at stake (say, for example, you have been out of work for several months, the severance pay from your old employer has run out, and your spouse is nagging you about the mortgage payment that is due the first of next month), it is very difficult indeed for your mind to tell your stomach and your nerve endings to "calm down, it's only an interview, it's not your life."

Rather than waste time focusing on your general demeanor or image as you walk into the interview room (we will talk about that in the next section), let us focus instead on your mind-set—what is going through your mind as you walk into the room and greet the interviewer.

It is my experience that you cannot control your feelings at a given moment; if you are thinking sad thoughts you cannot help but feel sad. By changing your thoughts, however, you can manipulate your feelings—how you perceive an event is as important (and sometimes, as we will see, more important) as the event itself. Politicians and their advisors often resort to *spin control*—presenting an event in the light most favorable to the politician or the light least favorable to his adversaries—in order to manipulate the public's perception of the politician and his policy goals. You, too, can (and should) resort to spin control to put your thoughts in the light most favorable to you before you begin a legal job interview; your feelings will follow your positive thoughts naturally, and you will present a positive image to the interviewer. Let us see how it is done.

Rule # 1: Make Believe You Already Have the Job

This rule is not as outrageous as it sounds at first, for in a way, you may have already passed the biggest hurdle in winning a legal job before you walk into the first interview. If you are applying for an advertised or posted position, or if you have made a contact through networking or through a headhunter, your potential employer has reviewed your resume, screened your credentials, and decided that your background and experience fit the job. Otherwise, why would the company or firm waste time interviewing you?

Sometimes the only question remaining at that point is whether you are better suited for the job than the others who have also passed this initial screening along with you. In other words, the company or firm has already screened out those whose credentials and experience are clearly not a fit for the job. What is now necessary is to screen in the candidate to whom an offer will be made (with perhaps a backup) and screen out the rest.

In such a situation your mind-set walking into the interview should be: "I've already got the job. My credentials and experience are a fit, otherwise why would they be wasting their time on me? I won't spend a lot of time rehashing my resume, and I won't ever be defensive about anything on my resume, because in all likelihood they have already figured out they can live with whatever weaknesses there may be in my background."

You have all heard about sports teams who go into a big game where they are highly favored over their opponents. About such a team it is often said that the game is theirs to lose, meaning that if they can keep their spirits up, maintain momentum and discipline at all times, and make a sincere effort to win, they should be able to do so easily. If, on the other hand, the favored team get lazy, allow themselves to be psyched out by the other team, or otherwise lose their discipline or momentum during the game, they stand a good chance of losing the game even though the other team isn't deserving of a victory.

You should think the same about yourself going into the "big game" of a legal job interview: "The job is already mine. I can only lose it by fouling up—by saying or doing something that annoys the interviewer or by revealing a significant weakness that the interviewer has no cause to suspect." We will examine some of the most common foul-ups in subsequent sections. The important thing now is to remember that when walking into a legal job interview you must not be overly concerned about selling yourself—like a telephone salesperson trying to sell you real estate in a swampland somewhere—but rather on not saying or doing anything that may cause the interviewer to think you are not a fit for the job.

Be assured, the interviewer is not on your side in this effort. He is looking for you to make such a mistake, because it makes his job much easier (you will recall from chapter 2 that this is the interviewer's primary goal: to make a decision he can easily defend in the shortest possible time and with the least amount of inconvenience or effort). The candidate who says or does something that displeases the interviewer effectively screens himself out of the competition, even though he may have the best credentials for the job and even though he may in reality be the most perfect fit. Some interviewers go out of their way to try to surface such screening-out information during an interview, and you must be sure at all times that the interviewer does not succeed!

Life is not fair this way. Often (in fact, I think most of the time), the winner in a legal job interview is not the best qualified candidate but simply the one who performed the best during the interviewing process. In other words, the victor is not often he who is best but he who has made the fewest mistakes—and isn't that after all a prime quality of the good lawyer, that he doesn't make mistakes when representing a client in court or drafting a legal document or negotiating a delicate business transaction? As a friend of mine who does a lot of interviewing for his firm puts it: "Sometimes we pick a person out of the pack simply because we can't think of anything bad to say about him—even though we're not wildly enthusiastic about him—and we can indeed say bad things about the other candidates."

Rule # 1 is not in itself a guarantee of success in a legal job interview. If, after several interviews, there remain several candidates, none of whom has made an interviewing mistake or otherwise screened himself out, the interviewer(s) must still make a decision and pick one. The result at that point may be a popularity contest or may hinge on an individual's unique strength in an area of critical importance to the job. Rule # 1 is, however, a guarantee that you will make it to the final cut and be among those considered.

Exception to the Rule: The Law School Placement Office Interview

There is an exception to rule # 1, which applies when you have signed up at your law school placement office to interview with a firm for your first legal job (be it a summer clerkship or your first job upon graduation). While you may be required to deposit your resume with the placement director a week or two before the interview date, usually the interviewer does not prescreen the resume and may be going into the interview with absolutely no idea of your credentials, background, or experience.

In such a situation you really cannot assume going in that you already have the job; indeed, you will probably spend most of the interview reviewing the items on your resume with the intent of demonstrating your fit for the job and the employer. If your grades are not up to snuff or you are not a law review type, you will probably be screened out before the interview even begins.

A better approach to follow in this situation is to tell yourself that for a specific type of employer (large firm, small firm, corporate legal department) all entry-level positions are alike, that one opportunity is as good as another, and it will only be a matter of time before you find a situation that will play to your strengths. There is an element of self-deception in this, but keep in mind that what you tell yourself is merely a tool designed to help you calm yourself down and keep the interviewing process in perspective and make a good first impression on the interviewer. Whether or not you internalize these beliefs after the interview is over is not important, because by then they will have served their purpose; they will have prevented you from looking like an uptight, worried, neurotic dweeb during the interview.

Rule # 2: Weave a Safety Net for Yourself, Even if You Have to Weave It Out of Thin Air

What about the feeling that you are under pressure to succeed in the interview? Or the feeling that "if I don't get this job it will be absolutely horrible—I'll end up on Skid Row?" Too much attention to these thoughts will make you appear anxious, worried, and pressured, and the interviewer will be turned off before you even open your mouth to say good morning. When you appear anxious, you make other people feel anxious. People are generally more responsive to your moods and feelings than you think. Have you noticed that whenever you are in a conversation with someone and you start talking faster and faster, they start talking faster and faster too? The same is true of emotions: if you appear awkward, you will make the interviewer feel ill at ease, and he will sooner or later begin to appear awkward. The interviewer does not enjoy this feeling of being awkward, he inwardly blames you for producing that feeling, and he will screen you out.

The Dating Game

It is one of the great ironies of interviewing that the candidates who display that they really need the job are never the ones who get it. Why? Well, let me ask you this. Was there ever someone in your life who developed a crush on you and followed you everywhere you went, making a nuisance of himself or herself trying to get your attention, and doing everything within his or her power short of committing a felony to get you to go out with him or her? If there was, tell me, how interested were you in that person?

Did you ever stop to think that that person would do anything for your affection, be more true and loyal to you than anyone else, and return your affection tenfold until the day he or she died? I'll bet you actually did at some point or other. But you still weren't interested, were you, you soulless heartbreaker? Instead of settling for the one you could get without lifting a finger, you spent your time trying to get the attention of someone who wouldn't even give you the time of day. And, pray tell, how did he or she treat you? Probably just the same way you were treating the poor slob who was tagging along everywhere after you with his or her tongue hanging down to his or her knees.

It is much the same with interviewing. The candidate who is most likely to get a job interview is the one the interviewer most likes but is not completely certain he can get. (All the good ones are taken!) The candidate he is least interested in is the one who fawns all over him and sends him a signal that he would do anything to get the job. (Desperate!) Why this is I don't know. But it is a fact of interviewing life.

Another possible reason for this, which should not be overlooked, is that the law is not a very emotional business.

A lawyer is expected to remain calm and detached at all times. This puts clients at ease, because if a lawyer looks worried, the client sees a jail cell or the poorhouse in his future. Lawyers are uncomfortable generally with people who display their emotions or who otherwise show that they cannot control their feelings. If a candidate appears overly eager or overly anxious, an interviewer is likely to think to himself, "If this person gets so wound up about a lousy job interview, can you imagine how he'll be in a tough courtroom situation? How will he deal with some of our crazier clients?"

This is not to say that you should send signals that you are not interested in the job you are interviewing for. Heaven forbid! That would be an instant screen out of the type you want to avoid at all costs. It does mean, however, that you have to stifle a certain amount of your enthusiasm for the job or the employer, even at the risk of appearing a trifle distant or lukewarm.

The Little White Lie

I worked a few years as a reporter for a major metropolitan daily newspaper before I started law school. That was years ago, but whenever I find myself thinking that a job interview is a do-or-die situation, I calm myself down by telling myself that if all else fails I can always go back to that newspaper (or another one) and write obituaries or feature articles for a while.

Now, I haven't the foggiest idea if I could in fact do such a thing; I probably would be considered overqualified for such a position by this time. But this little white lie that I have told myself does me a great deal of good. I usually do calm down and keep the interview in better perspective, and as a result I appear calmer and more relaxed, which puts the interviewer at ease and makes me appear more professional and mature.

This little white lie is what I mean when I say that you should weave a safety net for yourself, even if you have to weave it out of thin air. It will be much easier for you to believe (sincerely) that winning the job is not the most important thing in your life if you can persuade yourself that you do in fact have other options—that there is always something else you can do if all else fails and you don't get a job offer from anyone in the world. Think about something you would really like to do that is possible for you to do without a great deal of money or inconvenience—start a small business out of your home, for example, or become a late-night disc jockey for your local radio station, or write legal articles for your local newspaper.

Forget for the moment that the job wouldn't pay a decent living wage. Just concentrate on picking something that you could do well without much effort, that would give you an entry-level position without much effort, and that would be fun to do for a while. Once you have found it, make it your safety net—write it down on a little piece of paper, stick it in your wallet or purse (in a place where you can reach it easily and scan it while waiting for the interview to begin), and keep saying to yourself, "I'm not making a big deal of this. It would be nice to get the job, but if all else fails, I can always do X—I will not end up on the streets rummaging through garbage pails for my supper." Just don't fall too much in love with your safety net position, or you may just decide to give up practicing law altogether!

Rule # 3: Warm, Friendly, Smile, Low-Key

This is really a collection of rules, a mantra that I repeat to myself just before walking into a legal job interview. I have found it helpful in developing the right frame of mind, which in turn affects the image I present to the interviewer in a very positive manner. Let us look at each element of rule # 3 in turn.

Be Warm

It should go without saying that you should not come across as a cold fish. Your personal style should be warm and inviting, your stance relaxed without being limp. Your facial expression and body language should communicate to the interviewer, "Look, I am genuinely interested in this position, but I don't look upon this interview as a stressful situation, and neither should you. So let's get down to the business of getting to know each other."

Be Friendly

Without showing too much of your personality, you should signal to the interviewer that you genuinely like him, that you are the sort of person who would get along with just about anybody and win them over. As in other professions and walks of life, loners generally do not succeed in the law. Attracting and keeping clients requires as many people skills as technical lawyering skills, and no law firm or corporation wants to hire someone who will have to work behind closed doors all the time.

Smile

You should not forget to do this. Your smile should not be flashy or forced, but you must not forget to smile. Psychologists tell us that when we smile we unconsciously trigger happy thoughts and emotions that put our minds at ease; your actions in this regard do indeed influence your thoughts. If you do not have a natural smile, develop one! If necessary, tell yourself a favorite joke or remind yourself of a humorous or silly situation from your past as you walk in the door. Your slight laugh will come across as a natural smile.

Be Low-key

This is the most important element of rule # 3. You absolutely must not appear to be intense, uptight, or overly concentrated. You must send a signal to the interviewer that nothing really bothers you and that while you work well under pressure, you never let the pressure get to you. Far from being a turn-off, this sort of emotional detachment from the situation is a very positive sign that you are a mature, mentally healthy, well-adjusted professional.

The trick is to present a low-key image without appearing to be bored or uninterested. One way to avoid appearing too laid-back is to listen intently to the interviewer's every word, and make it a point not to sit too far back in your chair.

Applying the Rule

Once you have mastered rule # 3, you must make a mantra of it. Just as the door of the interview room swings open, you should repeat to yourself "warm, friendly, smile, low-key" over and over again. During the interview, if the interviewer has launched on a lengthy monologue about his employer or a favorite war story, you should occasionally repeat to yourself "warm, friendly, smile, low-key." Finally, as you stand to leave the interview room or walk with the interviewer down the hall to your next interview, the phrase "warm, friendly, smile, low-key" should be foremost in your mind.

Another helpful mnemonic device you can use to set yourself in the right frame of mind before a legal job interview is what I call the four Cs—Calm, Confidence, Courage, Control—with *control* being the most important. Not only are you going to be in control of your emotions, fears, and feelings, real or imagined, but you are also going to control the flow of information during the interview, in a way that will present you in the best possible light. You will learn the key ways of accomplishing this control over the interviewing process later in this chapter.

Rule # 4: Show a Personal Interest in the Interviewer

It is common for an inexperienced job candidate to begin an interview by rattling off every item on his resume or giving the answer to an anticipated question that has not been asked yet (or may never be asked). While it is natural for you to want to get down to business quickly, you must repress this natural desire. By giving in to it you send the interviewer an invisible signal that you want to "get this over with quickly" or worse yet, that you are an intense, self-absorbed neurotic who does not know how to get along with people.

You must take the time to get to know the interviewer personally; if the interviewer does not buy you as a person, he is not about to buy you as a lawyer. If the interviewer begins talking as you walk in the door (most lawyer/interviewers will start the conversation), listen intently to what is being said and forget for a moment your prepared lead-in or initial question. See if you can't think of a follow-up question to ask; doing this successfully shows the interviewer you know how to listen, you are keenly interested in what he said (which cannot but impress him), and you are able to focus on the moment without following an internal script. As we will see later in the chapter, the earlier you start directing the interview, the more likely it is you will succeed.

What if the interviewer does not begin talking as you walk through the door, but instead just sits there in stony silence, looking at your resume or just staring at you? If you have done your research on the interviewer as described in chapter 3, you should have found at least one common area of interest that you could use to begin the interview. I would begin by pointing out this area of interest and then asking a question based on it. For example, if your research has uncovered that the interviewer is an alumnus of your law school, you might say something like, "It must be interesting for you to come back to [name of law school] each year. Do you see any differences or any changes taking place since you were here?" This is small talk and accepted as such. But it shows that you are interested in the interviewer as a person without going out of your way to brownnose him, and it gets the conversation off to a relaxed start. Most importantly, it gets the interviewer to open up and start talking about something he cannot help but have something to say about.

Another approach is to highlight a shared interest, especially if you can do so by focusing on an object or event that is immediately present. For example, let's say that as you walk into the interviewer's office he is on the telephone talking to a client about a pending antitrust lawsuit. You have just taken an antitrust course and understand what the interviewer means when he refers on the telephone to a "possible Robinson-Patman claim." When the interviewer hangs up and apologizes for the delay, you may wish to say something like, "No, not at all, in fact I was quite interested in what you were talking about. I'm working on a paper on the Robinson-Patman Act right now, and your conversation sounded interesting. If I may ask, what is that case about?"

Or, if you see a model of a sailboat on his desk, you may wish to begin the interview by saying, "That model looks interesting. Are you a sailor?" The interviewer will then have no choice but to talk about a hobby he no doubt dearly loves (if he is a sailor) or (if he is not a sailor) explain how the sailboat model came to be sitting on his desk. Either way he will be talking about something that is of interest to him, and if you listen very carefully you will not have to worry about what to say next; his conversation will lead naturally to a follow-up question.

There is no better way to get someone to like you than to show (1) that you are interested in him as a person and are willing to spend some time getting to know him before you get down to business and (2) that you share a common interest, goal, or background. It bears repeating that human beings are attracted to people they perceive as being like themselves. Throughout the interview you should be emphasizing how the two of you are really quite similar people, and downplay any significant differences (such as ethnic background or law school grade point average) that may exist.

Rule # 5: Make 'Em Laugh

Let's face it, lawyers are not funny people. Their business is a serious one. People generally don't call their lawyers when they're having a nice day, and they will usually have little time or patience for levity. Nonetheless, there are few better ways to break the ice than to get the interviewer to laugh. There is an old saying among criminal lawyers that "a laughing jury never convicts." Similarly, a laughing interviewer cannot help but think you are a clever person if you can make him laugh during what is for him a stressful experience.

You should be very careful, however, how you go about making the interviewer laugh. Telling jokes (especially off-color ones) will not go over very well. Rather, a well-told humorous incident from your own past, especially one that highlights one of your personal or professional strengths, is the way to go. If your personality is such, however, that you are not comfortable with humor, it is best to avoid it altogether than risk making a fool of yourself.

Rule # 6: Warm Up for Your Audience

Before striding out on the stage of a comedy club or night spot, a stand-up comedian does not sit alone in his dressing room staring at the four walls. Instead, he will walk around talking to the backstage hands and the other entertainers, talking about anything that may come into his head. He is not doing this for idle amusement; he is warming up for his act, putting himself at ease, exercising his vocal cords, and pumping a little bit of adrenalin so that when he is announced and runs up on stage to take the microphone, he appears to do so naturally and without an awkward pause in the flow of the evening's entertainment.

While you should not come across as a stand-up comedian during a legal job interview, this warming up technique is one you should consider using. You should not stand or sit in the waiting area silently, staring at the four walls. This will make you more nervous, as when you are idle you are more likely to be besieged by unwanted, negative, self-defeating thoughts. Once you've had the chance to make your initial observations about the space (as described in chapter 3), try to talk to someone—anyone—in a casual, lighthearted manner, as this takes your mind off the immensity of the task ahead of you, calms you down, and enables you to practice your shtick before an audience of people who are not sitting in judgment over you.

I find that clerical staff are especially useful in this regard. If I am forced to wait outside the interviewer's office for a minute or two before the interview begins, I almost always strike up a conversation with the interviewer's secretary, asking questions about the office decor, the working environment, items on his desk that reveal a shared interest, and so forth.

If I am lucky, that person will reveal something about the boss that will provide me with a much-needed opener for the interview. I may, if I am really lucky, learn something about the interviewer that will help me decide if I want the job or not. I was once having such a conversation with the secretary of a man who was going to interview me, and at one point she said, "You know, would it be possible for you to wait another minute or two? His wife has been trying to reach him all day and I've had her on hold for 15 minutes." He then appeared, ushering me into his office, apologizing for the delay, and when I suggested that he should feel free to first take any telephone calls he had on hold, he said, "Oh, don't worry about that flashing light; I know who it is, and it can wait." Right away, I felt that this was probably not a person I would like to work for. If he treated his spouse that way, how would he treat me? But if I had not known this inside bit of information, who knows? I might have taken the job and found out the hard way.

YOUR PROFESSIONAL APPEARANCE

Before you open your mouth in a legal job interview, the interviewer will have an opportunity (however brief) to see how you look, how you dress, how you walk, and how you carry yourself. Since first impressions are lasting ones, you need to be very concerned about those fleeting first moments when the interviewer is sizing you up. This is not a dress for success book by any means, and you should follow closely the suggestions made by John Molloy in his two classic books—*Dress for Success* and *Women's Dress for Success*—which you can find in just about any bookstore. I have found, however, that there are a few special rules for lawyers who are interviewing with other lawyers, and they deserve special mention here.

Dressing for Success in the Legal Job Interview

The key word here is *dull*. Dull, dull, dull! The slightest hint of glitz, glamour, high fashion, or sexiness will usually be enough to displease a lawyer/interviewer. Remember that one of your goals is to appear low-key and understated during a legal job interview. Similarly, your look should be low-key and muted in both color and style. For both men and women, the preferred color scheme is the same: a navy blue or charcoal gray suit, a white shirt or blouse, and a maroon tie (either a solid maroon or a club tie with small—very small—repetitive designs on it).

While it is certainly true that different regions of the United States have different customs when it comes to business dress, you cannot go wrong with a conservative, buttoned-down look that says, "I am a professional; I take my work seriously." When in doubt, tone it down and take no chances. Remember that your goal is not to knock the interviewer's socks off with your highly developed ability to coordinate colors, but rather to avoid making a negative impression. Your clothing should be a neutral factor in the decision made about your fit for the job; ideally the interviewer should not even notice what you are wearing.

Regarding perfumes and aftershaves, the best smell in a legal job interview is no smell at all. Jewelry should be muted or nonexistent except of course for wedding or engagement rings.

What about a briefcase or other accessory? There is one school of thought that carrying a briefcase into an interview is a good idea, as it gives the interviewer an idea of how you will look when you walk into the firm (or company) each day. I personally do not subscribe to this theory; an interviewer knows that you do not walk around all day carrying a briefcase. I normally do not carry anything with me during an interview. I leave my briefcase in the closet by the reception area, along with my coat and umbrella (if it is raining). If the interviewer wants to see what I look like on the subway, he is welcome to escort me out of the office in person and watch while I put these things on.

I do, however, keep a spare copy of my resume with me. Many times the interviewer will not have this handy on his desk (or it will be buried beneath his many piles of paperwork), and it makes you look organized if you can spare him the indignity of tearing through the mess on his desk before you can begin the interview. Incidentally, it also prevents you from rehashing your resume verbally while the interviewer takes notes—an awkward, undesirable, and risky venture, because you want to be past the point where your credentials are being closely scrutinized.

Your Physical Appearance

It goes without saying that your body and face should be clean, your shirt and suit clean and pressed, your tie stainless, and your hair clean and brushed in a conservative style (no spikes or ponytails, gentlemen!).

In addition to the fact that you don't want your lawyer/interviewer to be distracted by your physical appearance, it is a prejudice of the lawyer's life in general that his appearance should not offend his clients. Your lawyer/interviewer will be mindful of this during the interview. Strange or unflattering glasses or dark (or orange!) tans can be easily avoided. Large moles can be removed, and crooked teeth can be fixed. Again, the emphasis is not on personal style or popular taste. For example, I personally happen to like beards (on men, anyway!) and sported a moustache in my youth. But most of the time facial hair is not acceptable, so it's better to be safe (and clean shaven) than sorry.

Only you can judge if your prospective employer is flexible enough to let you be yourself while on the job; generally, lawyers are much more tolerant of people's eccentricities than are other professionals. I have found, however, that long-term success in the legal profession often means carrying yourself in such a way that you alienate the fewest possible number of people. The decision is yours and yours alone, but if your grades are not top-notch, or you do not have enough portable business to sustain yourself, I suggest you err on the side of conformity for a while before you decide to set yourself apart from the madding crowd.

Habits and Body Language

Idiosyncrasies do not sit well with interviewers generally. If you have any tics or habits, such as biting your nails or fidgeting, you must learn to control these before entering the interview room. One good way to control your hands is to practice three standard positions—arms resting on your chair's arms with your hands holding onto (but not gripping for dear life) the ends of the armrests; hands folded in front of you; or one arm resting on the chair's arm while the other hand is resting on the opposite knee—and shift from one to the other periodically during the interview.

Psychologists tell us it is bad body language to cross your arms in front of you—such a position is essentially defensive and signals suspicion or distrust of what is being said. Accordingly, this is a position you should avoid during an interview. Do not fold your arms across your chest, for example, and do not wrap one arm around your waist while the other rests on the chair's armrest. Similarly, you should always face the interviewer head-on and not turn your left or right side toward him at any point.

How and Where to Sit

Your feet should remain firmly on the floor (no nervous tapping) and your posture should be roughly 90 degrees from the floor (no slouching over or leaning back in your chair).

A common interviewing strategy is to offer you a plush chair or sofa, while the interviewer retains a straight-backed chair. If you are like me, you will inevitably find yourself sinking lower and lower into the cushy chair's upholstery, such that the interviewer will be looking down at you throughout the interview. If given the choice, you should always sit in a straight-backed chair.

Some interviewing offices are set up in such a way that you and the interviewer have two seating options: you either will sit on one side of the interviewer's desk while the interviewer sits on the other, or there will be an arrangement of chairs and sofas that will create for awkward moments as each of you figure out where to sit. In the latter case my preference is to let the interviewer sit down first, and then pick a chair or sofa as close to the interviewer as possible in which I am facing 90 degrees away from the him (in other words, I am not looking at him straight on, nor are we facing the same direction). I find that this sends the desired signal that I am one of his kind of people (because we are not at odds with each other), while at the same time respecting the necessary formality of an interview situation (we are not sitting on the same side of the table, at least not yet). If there is more than one interviewer, I make sure that my back is not turned to anyone and that I am facing all of the interviewers as straight on as possible to avoid the ping-pong effect of turning this way and that as questions are asked. If the interviewers position themselves such that this is not possible, I usually determine which of the interviewers has the most clout and position myself in the strongest position relative to him. For example, if I am being interviewed by a partner and an associate, and the two position themselves opposite each other, I will sit in between them but with the chair moved to the partner's side so that the associate can look at me and the partner as if we were equals. I will be at my preferred 90-degree angle to the partner, while the partner will not be tempted to compare me with the associate as would be the case if the associate and I sat closely together.

Another example: if the partner and associate were to sit directly next to each other in what I call the united front formation, rather than sit directly across from them I would choose instead to sit at a 90-degree angle to the partner, on the opposite side of the partner from the associate. This usually forces the associate to adjust his position so as to break up the united front, since otherwise he cannot look at me straight on.

Now, you may think that some of this game of musical chairs is simply silly. You are, after all, being reviewed on the strength of your credentials and perceived fit for the job, right? What does it matter where you sit, for crying out loud?

Rather than disagree with you (frankly, much of this sort of thing is quite silly), I would simply point out that in many delicate international negotiations, in which war and peace may be at stake, the delegates (or their representatives) normally spend a great deal of time in determining the seating order. Obviously they consider it important that adversaries not be perceived by the press or public as friends or allies, and vice versa. They consider it important; why shouldn't you? The competition for legal positions is fierce these days, and you cannot afford to be screened out because of a silly thing having nothing whatever to do with what really counts: how good a lawyer you are (or have the promise of becoming).

Eye Contact

How much eye contact should you maintain with the interviewer? Generally, you should position yourself so that your face is always in the interviewer's plain view, facing him straight on. You should maintain eye contact as much as possible, especially when you are answering one of the interviewer's questions, as this is viewed as a sign of sincerity and openness. However, you should not stare at him too closely, or follow his glance wherever it may roam. At best, this will make the interviewer uncomfortable; at worst (and especially if the two of you are of opposite sexes), it may be ominously misread!

On the other hand, your eyes should not wander. A good solution is to allow your eyes to focus on points that are generally in the area of the interviewer's head, but without turning your head or otherwise appearing to be looking away from the interviewer.

This problem of eye contact becomes especially acute when there are multiple interviewers. On the one hand, you don't want to appear to be playing to one interviewer at the expense of another (you don't, after all, really know who has more clout). On the other hand, you don't want to seem like the spectator at a tennis or ping-pong match whose head moves perpetually back and forth while following the bouncing ball.

A good way to avoid this, as mentioned earlier, is to position your chair so that you are not caught directly between interviewers and can look in the general direction of both (or all), while allowing your glance to move to the person who is speaking at that moment. Another good way to strike the right balance (especially if you are caught in the middle of a ping-pong situation) is to look at the person who is talking and, if the other asks a question, tilt your head in the direction of the person speaking while looking at a point equidistant between the two interviewers. By doing this you appear to be thinking about your answer in a way that does not make either interviewer think you are ignoring him.

THE KEY RULE FOR SUCCESS IN A LEGAL JOB INTERVIEW

More than any other rule in this book, there is one rule you must keep foremost in your mind during a legal job interview. It is the key to success; disobeying or flaunting this rule is, in my opinion, the single biggest cause of being screened out in a legal job interview. It is a simple rule to remember and yet is difficult to apply in practice, both because it runs counter to a lawyer's nature and because it contradicts the advice given in countless books on interviewing (which, you will recall, are devoted to the professional interviewer or human resources executive, not the lawyer/interviewer). It takes a lot of guts to follow this rule, but I guarantee that your interviewing performance will improve dramatically if you discipline yourself to follow it rigorously.

So what is this miracle rule? I can state it many ways, but it all boils down to five simple words: SAY AS LITTLE AS POSSIBLE.

I call this the 20/80 rule: I do not consider any legal job interview a success if, upon reflection, I conclude that I have done more than 20 percent of the total talking, and the interviewer has done less than 80 percent.

Do you remember the story from chapter 1 of my two interviews with Firm A and Firm B? Do you recall that I thought I did wonderfully at Firm A, when in fact I was setting myself up for a quick rejection? Do you recall that I thought I did terribly during my afternoon of interviews at Firm B and ended up getting an offer from the head of the firm? Did you wonder why that happened?

Well, now you know why! Because at Firm A, I held court like the czars; I chattered my head off at each interview, selling and selling and selling my credentials and experience and hardly let the interviewers get a word in edgewise. They probably thought I was such an egotistical jerk that I deserved to be rejected from society at large, not merely their firm! By contrast, at Firm B I let the interviewers do all of the talking, for the simple reason that I was not adequately prepared and didn't want to let it show.

The lawyers at Firm B probably thought I was fascinated by their war stories and perspectives on the practice of law, which flattered them no end and led them to believe not only that I was an incredible conversationalist but had tremendously sound judgment to boot! They probably thought they had to rush to make me an offer or else I would be gobbled up by more than one of their competing firms!

Most of the books on interviewing stress that, if an interview is handled correctly by the interviewer, the candidate will do the lion's share of the talking. That way he gets to open up and show the interviewer what he is really all about so that the interviewer can make in-depth judgments about the candidate's poise, character, judgment, commitment, and above all, fit. This is because these books are all about interviewing with professional interviewers: personnel people and human resources executives who have been intensely trained in the art of interviewing and know how to do it well.

In contrast, in a legal job interview you are being interviewed by a lawyer who has not been so trained. By doing the lion's share of the talking, you increase dramatically the odds that you might screen yourself out. Why? There are two reasons.

For the first reason, we can take cues from none other than Dale Carnegie. In his classic book, *How to Win Friends and Influence People,* written almost a century ago, Carnegie stressed the need to make other people feel important by really listening to what they have to say and not burdening them with the sound of your voice.

Now, in the legal job interview your interviewer is a lawyer, and lawyers—more than most members of the human race—like to be listened to. The more you talk, the less interested in you the lawyer/interviewer becomes. Why? Because the surest way to win someone over as a friend and ally is to show a genuine and sincere interest in the things that matter most to him. The more interest you show in the interviewer and his affairs, the more interested he will be in you. He will most likely perceive you as his kind of person and will remember you fondly as "the person who showed such a keen interest in my stamp collection and my big case against the local electric utility." In addition, you are signaling to him that you are willing to do things his way instead of yours—you are flexible and will easily adapt to whatever habits, style, or culture your potential employer may want from its employees.

This is key. You will recall from chapter 2 that lawyers by nature are not risk takers; they tend to shoot for the safest and least risky course—the easy single instead of the long-odds home run. This is no criticism of lawyers; this is what they are trained to do! How would you feel about your tax lawyer if he told you, "If you take this course of action, you stand a 99 percent chance of being audited by the IRS. But let's go ahead anyway"? Something tells me you would not praise him for his innovative thinking and willingness to take risks.

By asserting or selling yourself too strongly—by talking too much—you send a clear signal to the interviewer that you are more interested in doing things your way, and there are few better ways to lose status in any organization than to let them think that you are a loner, not a team player, or someone who is not flexible in his attitudes and behavior on the job. Conversely, by saying little during an interview, you demonstrate that you are a good listener who is willing to do things the right way—meaning, of course, the interviewer's way—and take the time to find out what that right way is before shooting your big mouth off or taking precipitous action.

You may be saying to yourself that this is all contrary to common sense; aren't you supposed to make an effort to impress the interviewer, as all of the interview books recommend? Aren't you supposed to demonstrate that you stand head and shoulders above all the other candidates for the job? Aren't you supposed to sell yourself?

THE IMPORTANCE OF BEING LAID-BACK

While you should appear genuinely interested in the position and in the interviewer, you must not get carried away. Thus, the way to act during a legal job interview is what I call *laid-back*: your facial expression should be relaxed and not too expressive; your speech should be low in volume and pitch and should avoid strong inflections (a cultivated monotone—what one lawyer friend of mine calls the "lawyer's whisper"—is desirable here); your posture should not convey an image of intensity; your walk should be slow and deliberate, like a cat treading carefully to avoid alerting his prey; and your dress should be understated and perhaps even a little dull.

The other important reason why talking a lot can screen you out in a legal job interview has to do with how people, in general, recall people and events. Let's say that you and I meet at a street corner and that we discuss 10 topics—any topics at all. Let's further suppose that we agree warmly on 9 of these topics, but we disagree strongly about the 10th. We part company and meet again at that same street corner a year later after not having seen each other at all during the interim. We may not remember any of the 9 topics we agreed about during our earlier discussion, but we are sure to remember the 10th!

As a short digression, I submit that this is the reason that politicians are so noncommital when making statements about what they will do once they are elected to office, and fail to take strong stands on the issues. If I am running for office and you agree generally with my views on defense spending, the mortgage foreclosure crisis, aid to the homeless, and the need for lower taxes, but you disagree violently with my views on abortion, tell me, what are you going to be thinking about when you pull the curtain behind you in that voting booth? If you are like most people, all you will think when you see my name underneath the voting lever is "that idiot Ennico!" and you will pass me over in favor of another candidate. As my father used to tell me when I was a boy, "Better to keep your mouth shut and let people think you are a fool than to open your mouth and prove it."

When the lawyer/interviewer reflects upon the many candidates he has seen during his recent visit to XYZ Law School or reviews the many resumes sitting on his desk after having been distracted by a client's business for the past week or two, he will likely remember very few details about the candidate: what he looked like, what they talked about, what his grades were, whether he was a member of law review, and so forth. He will, however, remember anything you said that sounded wrong or off key to him or that signaled a less-than-perfect fit with the position or the firm. Simply put, the less you say, the less likely you will say something the interviewer will remember negatively.

A friend of mine once blew a legal job interview with a small firm in a suburban town when the interviewer asked how he felt about smaller firms in general. As part of my friend's answer—to buttress his point that it was often difficult to maintain a collegial, friendly working atmosphere in a large law firm—he inadvertently expressed the opinion that it is difficult for a law firm to operate in a collegial manner once there are more than 50 attorneys in the firm. My friend of course had done his homework and knew that the firm had significantly less than that number. Well, as it turns out my friend's interviewer was an ambitious sort whose goal was to see the firm grow to 100 lawyers—my friend's opinion was the last thing he wanted to hear. The interview ended abruptly at that point; my friend had said the one thing the interviewer needed to hear in order to screen him out.

At some point in the process of selecting someone for a new position, the people who have interviewed the candidates usually sit down around a table and compare the merits of each candidate. In such situations, the winner is very often not the person with the most impressive credentials or achievements, but rather the person with the best interview. By following the 20/80 rule, the lawyer/interviewer at least will not be able to say anything bad about you, because he was so busy talking that he neglected to ask you about you! He will then be forced to make his decision based on what is on the piece of paper in front of him, which usually will be skewed in your favor (you wouldn't dare say anything negative about yourself in your resume, would you?).

A corollary of the 20/80 rule should be mentioned in passing: if the interviewer is selling you, shut up. If you sense during the interview that the interviewer is going out of his way to sell you on his employer or his practice, and especially if he is doing so openly, congratulations! You've got it made! He wants you and he is letting you know you have sold him on your credentials, your experience, and your personality. There is nothing more for you to do! So don't blow it by opening your mouth, getting carried away with your success, and blurting something out that is going to turn the interviewer around or make him doubt his judgment.

ASKING THE RIGHT QUESTIONS

So what should you say during an interview? Obviously, if the interviewer asks you a direct question, you must answer it— I am not counseling that you be evasive. Answer the question in the most direct, concise, and short (short, short, short) manner possible, giving your answer the most positive spin you can. Once you have done so, then you should either shut up or (preferably) ask the interviewer a question.

Think of the legal job interview as a verbal tennis match. Like many of the great tennis players, your strategy is to keep the other player running back and forth, back and forth, from one side of the court to the other, so intent on returning your perfectly placed volleys that he forgets to go back on the offensive. *Your* volleys are your questions that you have carefully prepared in advance and committed to memory, after having thoroughly research the employer and the interviewer as recommended in chapter 3.

Whenever you find yourself in an awkward silence during a legal job interview, the solution is for you to ask the interviewer a question, not volunteer more information on something you may have already beaten to death. Keep the interviewer talking about himself, his practice, his great victory in a recent case, his great defense of the serial killer, his hobbies and personal interests, whatever! But keep him talking!

And while the interviewer is talking, don't forget to listen to what he is saying. Your goal here is not to kill time, but to make the interviewer open up so much that he accidentally leaks some information about the employer and its practice that may actually be useful to you. If the interviewer confides that he is so busy that he has little or no time for outside interests, that will tell you more about the employer and its culture than a 100-page *Martindale-Hubbell* entry ever will. While the interviewer is talking, you should be listening, not thinking about the next question to ask; if you listen carefully and closely enough, the next question can suggest itself to you without any effort on your part. And if you can't think of a follow-up question, you will pick out another from your memorized list of questions and ask it as soon as the interviewer finishes answering this one (if indeed he ever does).

As you can see, to keep the interviewer talking and genuinely interested in the one-way discussion, your questions must be the right ones. We will discuss in this section how to go about asking the right questions; chapter 7 will discuss some strategies for *answering* some commonly asked interviewer questions in the right way.

The right question in a legal job interview has three characteristics: (1) it must be pertinent to your twin goals of getting the interviewer on your side and establishing your perfect fit for the job, (2) it must not be too direct for fear of turning the interviewer off, and (3) it must put you in the best possible light.

The Question Must Help You Achieve Your Goals

What do we mean when we say the question must be pertinent to your twin goals of getting the interviewer on your side and establishing your perfect fit for the job? In asking a question, you are seeking either to impress the interviewer with the depth of your research or your shared experience, or you are seeking information you can use to show the interviewer how perfect you would be for the job. If a question does not serve either (or both) of these goals, it should not be asked.

You may be intently curious about weather conditions in the city where the interviewer's firm is located, but if you ask, "Tell me, Mr. So-and-So, what was it doing in XYZ City when you left this morning?" the interviewer cannot help but wonder where you are heading with this small talk. A better way to satisfy your curiosity is to watch the Weather Channel, or consult *USA Today*.

The Question Must Not Be Too Direct

While there is certain information about the employer's style and culture you simply must know in order to make an intelligent career decision, there are some things you cannot find out about by asking a direct question. For example, if you were to ask the interviewer, "Tell me, is your firm a sweatshop?" the interviewer would think you a total clod, because any firm in which he is a partner is definitely not a sweatshop and because you have just sent him a signal that you are not willing to work hard to learn your profession.

A better way to obtain the information you want, without risking a turn-off, is to ask indirect questions designed to elicit statistical information, such as the following:

- Are there any expectations as to the number of hours a first-year associate must work at your firm?
- Are you satisfied with the amount of personal time you and your colleagues have at this point in your lives?
- Are you satisfied with the amount of associate turnover your firm has experienced in the past few years?

Similarly, you should avoid questions about the firm's weaknesses and sore points, even if you think you can phrase them in a positive manner. Don't ask questions that are guaranteed to make the interviewer feel ill at ease, such as, "How is your firm handling that massive legal malpractice judgment that was rendered against you last year?" or "Is it true what I read in last week's *Fortune* magazine that your company is planning on a major downsizing of staff later this year?" Better ways to handle these questions are to phrase them as follows:

- How does your firm handle quality control as a general matter? Is there much close supervision of associates in the early years?
- What is your company's overall strategy for adding or reducing legal staff this year?

Note that these phrasings of the same questions are more general and value neutral and give the interviewer more latitude in putting a positive spin on the answer. Just be sure to listen to the answers closely.

The Question Must Make You Look Good

Finally, you must keep in mind that by asking questions you are interested not only in eliciting information from the interviewer, you are also trying to impress the interviewer with your intelligence, tact, and judgment. If a question does not make you look good, there is no point in asking it.

What sorts of questions will make you look good? Generally, there are two kinds: questions that play to the interviewer's "hot buttons" (such as a special interest or current problem— something the interviewer could talk about for hours); and skillful, original questions that the other 25 candidates have *not thought to ask*. An example of the hot button question is: "Mr. So-and-So, I see that you chair the state bar association's Blue Sky Law Committee. Tell me, what do you think of the current proposal in Congress to develop uniform standards for state blue sky laws?" An example of the skillful, original question is: "Mr. So-and-So, I see that your company is affiliated with a French financial institution with substantial interests in the Middle East. Tell me, will your company be involved at all in helping Iraq get back on its feet?"

The answers to these questions may, of course, be irrelevant to the position you are applying for. Their purpose, however, is to show the interviewer you have done your homework and are thinking about the same things that keep him awake at night. At the very least, he will know that you don't ask the same questions of every interviewer.

General Interview Questions

The key to asking good questions is to do your research as recommended in chapter 3, ask yourself if each question satisfies all three characteristics of the right interview question, and then memorize the question so that you can introduce it naturally and gracefully during the interview.

With the understanding that there are no good form questions for a legal job interview, here are some that I believe at least fit all three categories. Conform them to your own style of speaking and your own interests.

If I Was to Start Working in This Position Today, What Sorts of Projects Would I Be Working On?

I find this is a better question than "What skills are needed for this position?" because it focuses the interviewer on the tasks he needs done right now and gives you a much more detailed sense of the level of responsibility and client contact you can expect from the position. By asking follow-up questions about specific transactions, research projects, or cases, you can get quite a bit of mileage out of this one.

When You Think about Your Practice and Where It's Going, What Sorts of Things are You Happiest About?

Note that this question parallels that favorite of legal job interviewers: "What do you consider your strengths?" or "What is your greatest strength?" By asking this question you have simply turned the table on the interviewer, in what I believe is a fair and nonthreatening way. By getting the interviewer to open up about his own personal feelings about the practice of law in general (and the practice at his current employer), you can learn a great deal about how you will probably feel once you have reached the interviewer's level. You also send a signal to the interviewer, without saying so, that you are seriously considering being someday in his shoes, which any interviewer will find flattering.

Note that you should avoid asking the converse of this question—"When you think about your practice and where it's going, what are you most worried about?"—because it focuses the interviewer on a negative that will inevitably be transferred to you. A better way to ask this question, if you absolutely must, is: "Do you have any concerns at the moment about where your practice is going?"

Is There a Specialty You Don't Currently Have In-House That You Would Like to Develop?

This question has two purposes. The first is to learn about that part of the employer's practice that is most likely to experience growth over the next few years. You may also get a sense of the employer's weaknesses or if their clients' businesses aren't faring so well; for example, a sudden interest in bankruptcy work could spell trouble for the employer in the long run.

The second purpose is a bit more insidious: you are sending the lawyer/interviewer two very positive signals—that you are a market driven attorney who is willing to adapt his skills to his clients' changing needs and that you are interested in becoming one of the young attorneys who help the employer develop and grow into the desired area of practice. With a little bit of research, you may be able to answer this question yourself before the interview begins, and thus be ready to follow up with a brief summary of the work you have done in the desired area.

If You Had to Narrow It Down to One Thing, What Do You Think Is the Key to Success in This Position (or for An Entry-Level Position, "The Key to Success to Getting Ahead in Your Organization")?

The interviewer's answer to this question will tell you a great deal about the employer's culture and its image of itself. Don't expect to hear the truth, but listen closely anyway. If the interviewer stresses the ability to get along well with people, you know that politics are very important to getting ahead. If, on the other hand, the interviewer emphasizes the ability to work hard and get the job done, you know the place is a sweatshop where there will be little or no time for politics.

Specific Interview Questions

Some questions for specific positions are listed below, divided into important subtopics. These come with a stern

warning that they should rarely if ever be asked in precisely this form—you risk appearing packaged, and this will
displease the lawyer/interviewer. You should tailor these
questions to the circumstances of the particular employer
and interviewer, as they are designed to elicit extremely
important information.

Again, these general questions will need to be supplemented
by a lengthy list of job-specific and employer-specific questions
that you will generate in the course of your research.

Questions for Law Firm Positions

- Clients

    o What is the firm's client base and how (if at
      all) has it changed over the past 10 years?
    o What changes in the client base do you fore-
      see in the future?
    o What areas of practice is the firm most known
      for?
    o Is it a boutique firm with only a handful of
      specialties, or does it have a more diverse range
      of specialties in-house?
    o What is the culture associated with the
      specialty?

- Attrition

    o What is the turnover rate for associates after
      the first three years? The first five?
    o In each of the past five years, how many
      associates have been made partner as a rough
      percentage of the total number of associates

who were considered for partnership positions? (I find that this question generates more useful information than simply asking about the firm's partner-to-associate ratio, since the latter does not take into account changes in the firm's practice or client base.)

o Generally, where do those associates who have been passed over tend to find work once they leave the firm?

- Job characteristics and responsibilities

  o How important are business-generating skills in determining whether an associate will be made a partner?

  o What does the firm do in terms of training associates in their assigned duties? (For an entry-level position, you are probably more concerned about the quality of the education you will receive there than with your prospects of making partner, which is a long way in the future.)

  o If the firm needs to grow into new areas of practice, will they do so by retraining their associates or by hiring laterals from other firms (or merging with another firm that practices in the desired area)?

  o How are the partners and associates divided into teams?

  o To how many partners and senior associates will an associate have to report on each team?

- Company culture

  - o Do the partners of the firm generally get along well?
  - o Will the partners that head up a particular team be likely to agree on those matters that are most important to the associate, such as the quality of his work (reinforced by periodic reviews), his training and professional development, the number of desired billable hours, and the need for the associate to become involved in outside activities?
  - o What is the firm's culture? Is it aggressive, polished, "white shoe," low-key?
  - o Is there a tolerance for a diversity of associates in terms of race, gender, ethnicity, and so forth? How tolerant is the firm of an individual's eccentricities?

- Company image

  - o Does the firm have long-standing ties to a particular charity or political party?
  - o Does the firm believe that public service or community legal work is important?
  - o Have any of the partners served in government or other nonlegal appointments?
  - o How important is the bottom line to the firm? (It is always important, but is it the only thing that is important?)

Questions for Corporate Legal Positions

- Clients (corporation's employees)

  - o What is the key to success in winning the confidence of the businesspeople?

o Is the legal department highly or poorly regarded within the organization?

o Is inside counsel expected to lead the businesspeople, or is the inside counsel's role limited to counseling the businesspeople and letting them make the final decisions?

o Who are the company's outside counsel, and how strong are the company's ties to each firm? (There will usually be more than one firm depending on the type of work involved, and if the general counsel came from Firm X, you can be sure Firm X will always get at least a certain amount of work from the company.)

o Is the company looking to change its relationships with outside counsel in any way?

o Are there any areas in which the company's businesspeople believe they are not being adequately served by existing outside counsel?

o Between inside and outside counsel, who is expected to take the lead on transactions?

o Is inside counsel expected to attend every meeting and negotiating session?

o Is the inside counsel expected to manage the outside counsel's costs?

• Job characteristics and responsibilities

o Is the position more of a work position or a managing position? (Inside counsel's job is primarily to do the technical legal work on smaller matters, and the larger matters are handled by outside counsel. Or inside counsel is expected to know only a little about a lot of things and focus his energies instead on managing the company's relationships with outside counsel and participating in company business decisions.)

- Company culture

  o If the position is with a corporate subsidiary, how do the legal departments at the parent and subsidiary levels interface?
  o How much freedom of operation is allowed to the subsidiary's attorneys?

Questions for Government Agencies

- Clients (government agencies)

  o What is the agency's mandate from Congress (or the state legislature), and how has it changed over the years (i.e., is the agency's authority expanding or shrinking)?
  o Upon which aspects of the agency's mandate are the senior lawyers currently focusing their efforts? (Rarely are all of an agency's regulations enforced with equal zeal at all times.)
  o Are there areas in the agency's mandate in which the senior lawyers feel more enforcement effort is needed?

- Job characteristics and responsibilities

  o Are lawyers at the agency expected to play a role in expanding or clarifying policy? For example, if the agency receives a request for an administrative ruling which evidences a hole in the agency's regulatory structure, how involved will the staff lawyer become in this process?

o Do staff lawyers ever become involved in the legislative committees that draft laws which affect the agency's mandate?

o What is the average tenure in office of lawyers at the agency? Where do they tend to go and why do they leave?

- Company culture

  o Whom does the agency regard as its primary constituents?

  o Does it tend to cozy up to the people it regulates, or is it a watchdog that doesn't give an inch when interpreting its regulations and its mandate?

  o Does the current governmental administration have any expectations about how strong or lax an enforcement effort will be made by the agency? If it does, has it provided the agency with adequate support in achieving the administration's goal?

HANDLING THE INTERVIEWER'S QUESTIONS

Chapter 7 will give you some strategies for answering the most common interview questions. In this section I want only to highlight that your answers must be direct and end either in your silence or in a question for the interviewer.

I try to anticipate the interviewer's questions (and after a few interviews, this will become quite easy as the same questions tend to come up time and again) and prepare in my mind a response that will take no more than 15 seconds. If I find myself taking more than 15 seconds to answer a particular question, I will stop and ask the interviewer, "Am I reading your question correctly?" This gets the interviewer talking again, if only for a brief moment, and gives me the chance to obtain a clearer focus on what he's driving at. When the ball returns to my court, I make a very short reply and follow up with a question.

The Curveball

What do you do if the interviewer asks you a question and you really haven't the foggiest idea of what the answer should be? Most interviewing books will tell you to buy a second or two by saying something like, "That's an interesting question. I would have to think about that for a moment," and I heartily endorse that approach.

But what if you still can't come up with an answer? First, don't panic. The interviewer may want to know how you handle yourself in a difficult situation. If you try to fudge it, you will screen yourself out of the interviewing process: no lawyer likes to hear baloney from a client or a junior attorney. Rather than guess wrong, my preferred approach is to try to find out where the interviewer is headed. I may say something like, "That's an interesting question. Tell me, what is it about my background or experience that you are especially concerned about (or that you are especially interested in knowing more about)?" Usually this will signal to the interviewer that I am slightly confused by his question, and he will take some pains to clarify his intentions. If I listen closely enough, I usually will be able to figure out what he is looking for and be able to give it to him.

What if this does not work? I keep trying to clarify the question. I may repeat it in a slightly different fashion, using words that bring it closer in form to a question I am prepared to answer, and ask the interviewer if that is what he means to ask (I am careful of course not to appear to be evading the question). Under no circumstances, however, will I guess at an answer. If all else fails, and I can't figure out where the interviewer is headed, I may say something like, "You know, Mr. So-and-So, I really haven't given that much thought; I guess I didn't think anyone would be interested. I'd like to think about your question a bit and give you an answer later in the day. Will that be all right with you? I'd rather take the time to give you the right answer than blurt out something which won't be useful to you." And I always follow up on my promise to get back to him later in the day.

At best, I have satisfied his concern that I am not the sort of lawyer to shoot from the hip and answer difficult questions without doing the necessary homework. At worst, he will think that I am not sufficiently fast on my feet and screen me out, but at least I will now know another interview question for which I must have a ready answer.

Incidentally, I keep a file of recurring questions and an outline of my preferred answer to each one. Why reinvent the wheel each time you go out into the job marketplace?

There is one situation in particular in which you may find yourself at a loss for words—when the interviewer asks you a technical question about an area of law or practice in which you are holding yourself out as having some expertise. Chapter 7 will give you some advice on handling that very delicate situation (which, by the way, does not commonly occur; most lawyer/interviewers will take your resume at its word).

DEALING WITH NEGATIVE QUESTIONS

Once in a while, especially if your lawyer/interviewer is a litigator or trial attorney, you may find yourself the focus of a negative or adversarial interview. This is one in which all of the interviewer's questions appear to be designed to put you down or make you reveal unflattering or negative information about yourself, and it can be a truly terrifying experience. Even in a normal job interview, you may encounter one or two questions in which the interviewer appears to be less than impressed with something in your background or experience.

If you should ever be subject to such an interview, or if such a question should arise, keep in mind that things are not usually as they seem. In most cases the interviewer doesn't really think you are a jerk and isn't prejudiced against you before you walk into the room. Otherwise, why would he be taking the time to talk to you? Remember, your mental attitude should be that you already have the job before you walk in the door.

In situations where the tone of the entire interview is negative, the interviewer's purpose is not to humiliate you—although if you are not careful he may well succeed, since litigators are very good at cross-examining people and tearing apart their prepared stories—but rather to see if you are tough enough to survive in what he believes is a rough practice, a difficult environment, or an aggressive culture. In the situation where the overall tone of the interview is positive but the interviewer asks one or two negative questions, what is usually happening is that the interviewer has surfaced one or two things on your resume that he thinks he will have trouble selling to his partners or colleagues. He wants you to tell him what he should tell these people when they express their concern about these particular things.

Whatever you do in this situation, there are three important rules to keep in mind. First, don't be defensive. By reacting to the question with surprise, shock, or horror, you send a signal to the interviewer that you had something to hide and (shucks!) the interviewer has discovered the skeleton in your closet. Your first response to such a situation probably should be something like, "I anticipated that you would ask me about that." This puts the interviewer at ease and tells him that he probably won't have too difficult a job explaining this one difficult item. Also, be sure to keep your answer as short as possible. The more you make a big deal out of the negative item, the more the interviewer will too.

Second, remember that no one can intimidate you without your consent. You didn't go to law school because you wanted to be a shrinking violet. The legal profession is tough, combative, aggressive, and downright dirty at times. Show the interviewer that you can take the pressure without losing your cool. Remain calm at all times, but be sure to be assertive about your strengths, your achievements, and the positive aspects of your resume. In fact, if you sense that the interview is going to be entirely negative, you are free to ignore the interviewer's specific questions to a certain extent.

A simple example will illustrate the point. Let's say you know something about cars, and I sell you my old used car with a promise that it will get 30 miles to a gallon on the highway. You don't ask me about the state of the brakes, and I have no reason to tell you anything about the brakes because I don't notice anything wrong with them. Two weeks later you call me on the telephone and tell me the brakes on my old car are worn through and need to be replaced immediately. Of course if I value your friendship I will make some accommodation. But if I don't know you from a hole in the wall, and if I have reason to believe you should have known what you were doing when you bought the car, one perfectly valid response to your telephone call is for me to smile and ask, "But tell me, are you getting 30 miles to the gallon on the highway?" In other words, just because a person has asked you a leading question does not mean you have to give him a direct answer; you can counter a negative with a positive.

Third, in answering an interviewer's question you never, ever, ever volunteer negative information about yourself. Even if the lawyer/interviewer accuses you of having done something in your past that you know darn well is true, you never admit this to the interviewer. When this happens your preferred response is not to deny that it happened but to explain it in a low-key, off-the-cuff manner, in a way that any reasonable interviewer will find plausible, and then turn the interviewer's focus back on himself as quickly as possible. (I have observed that people who like to engage in adversary interviews are also people who love to hear themselves talk.)

If, for example, the interviewer asks, "Isn't it true, Mr. Candidate, that you have spent only an average of six months on each of your last three jobs?" it is much better to say something like, "Well, I'm sure you know this industry has had a rough time of it in the current recession; all three of my last employers went through substantial downsizings and when you're the last hired, you tend to be the first to be laid off. Isn't this your experience, Mr. So-and-So?" That's a much better response than, say, "Yes, Mr. So-and-So, you're right. I guess that makes me look like a job hopper or an incompetent, huh?" Appealing to an interviewer's sympathy and compassion is not usually a good strategy.

The best strategy when dealing with negative questions is to turn the question into a positive statement about yourself. For example, the lawyer/interviewer may ask you something like, "I see from your data sheet, Mr. Candidate, that you have been divorced three times; not much of a family man, are you?" (Incidentally, I think any interviewer who asks this kind of question in such a blatant manner is opening himself and his employer up to a lawsuit, if not a punch in the mouth; I am using this example because it is clear, not because I think it is a real-world question). You could say something like, "Well, Mr. So-and-So, my spouses haven't been too tolerant of my long hours at the office, it's true. It's really hard to find someone who really understands my commitment to the law and my total involvement in my work—I feel I can't let go of the problem until I am satisfied I have found the right answer. Tell me, how do you manage to reconcile career and family life in your demanding practice?" (Note that by answering in this fashion, you may make the interviewer start to wonder if he is as committed to the law as he thinks he is.) Not every situation, of course, lends itself to this approach, but if you can pull it off it is the legal job interviewing equivalent of the grand slam home run.

HANDLING THE AWKWARD SILENCE

It happens every once in a while; you have answered an interviewer's question, keeping your answer short, concise, and to the point. You then wait for the interviewer to say something or ask the next question. But nothing happens. The interviewer simply nods his head and encourages you to go on or just sits there like a statue and glares at you. Several awkward seconds pass and you frantically start thinking of ways to resume the dialogue. You have reached an impasse; neither you nor the interviewer seems capable of getting the interview going again.

I have never fully figured out why this happens so often in legal job interviews, but awkward silences are part of the game you must learn to play. As best as I can figure, there are three possible reasons for an awkward silence, in decreasing order of likelihood:

1. The interviewer is playing a game with you to test your poise in dealing with an awkward situation.
2. The interviewer's people skills are not well developed and he simply does not know what to say either.
3. The interviewer has fallen asleep with his eyes open (or, in one case that actually happened to a friend of mine, suffered a massive stroke and died) during your last answer.

Whatever the reason, there is a simple two-step strategy that will help you overcome the awkwardness and get the conversation going again in a way that makes you look like a seasoned professional.

Step one is to simply say nothing: look at the interviewer and wait for him to say something. Don't be afraid to let a few seconds pass in this fashion, as the awkwardness is mutual and the interviewer will be just as eager as you are to get things going again. What you don't want to do at any cost is to start babbling about anything and everything just to end the awkward silence. Remember the cardinal rule of legal job interviewing: SAY AS LITTLE AS POSSIBLE.

You have already answered the interviewer's last question to your satisfaction (and probably to his as well). If he wants you to expand upon your answer, let him give you an idea of what he wants. Just stare at him for a few seconds.

If after a few seconds the silence remains unbroken, it is time to resort to step two: ask the interviewer one of your prepared questions. Don't worry that the question is unrelated to the previous topic of discussion. Your goal here is to turn the initiative back where it belongs—in the interviewer's hands—and get him to start talking again. Most interviewers (especially in the second scenario described above, where the interviewer doesn't know what to talk about either) will be delighted or relieved at this approach, as it is exactly what a lawyer would do if a client clammed up on him during a counseling session.

If you sense that your interviewer has fallen asleep during the last answer, there is one sure way to find out: remain silent for a moment or two, and if there appear to be no signs of life in the interviewer, clear your throat sharply and loudly. If that does not produce a response, you may wish to say, in a fairly loud voice, "Mr. So-and-So, would you like me to expand at all on my previous answer?"

If there is still no response, you should begin to suspect cardiac arrest. (My friend left the office, walked calmly up to the late interviewer's secretary, and said, "Excuse me, ma'am, but I believe there's something wrong with Mr. So-and-So; could you please have a look at him with me? I think he's passed out." And no, I do not know whether or not my friend was offered the job.)

CLOSING THE INTERVIEW

Just as the most hazardous parts of an airline flight are the take-off and the landing, so the most awkward parts of a legal job interview are the beginning (where you are greeting the interviewer and trying to establish a personal rapport with him) and the end (where you are taking your leave and trying to end the interview on a positive note). Here are some simple rules to remember when a legal job interview comes to an end.

Rule # 1: Let the Interviewer Decide When the Interview Is Over

If your interview is scheduled to last 15 or 30 minutes, remember that time schedules are not graven in stone: if the interviewer runs over his allotted time (and this happens often), don't be fool enough to tell him so—let him ramble on with his interminable war story until the next interviewer (or more likely the legal personnel coordinator) comes by and reminds him of your schedule. Never be the one to terminate the interview—it sends a signal to the interviewer that you really did not enjoy talking to him.

Rule # 2: Express Your Enthusiasm for the Job and for the Interviewer

A good closing statement, modified as always to reflect your speaking habits, is: "I've really enjoyed meeting you, Mr. So-and-So. You have a wonderful practice here at Dewey Cheatham & Howe, and I would love to be a part of it." This closes the interview on an upbeat note, comforts the interviewer that he has not said anything to turn you off to the position, and sets you apart from those (and they are many) who do a good job of interviewing but fail to tell the interviewer that they want the job.

Rule # 3: If the Interviewer Escorts You, Keep Him Talking

If the interviewer walks you on to your next interview appointment, or to the door at the end of the day, be sure to continue talking to him. The interview is formally over, but there is no rule that says you cannot continue asking pertinent questions or make small talk with the interviewer right up to the final handshake. Continuing the conversation in an informal way signals to the interviewer that you are really a decent individual, confirms that what the interviewer saw during the formal interview session is the way you are in real life, and underscores your enthusiasm for the position.

A Word about Handshakes

You probably already know that your handshake must be firm but not bone crushing, and should not involve the sort of vigorous arm movement you would use in pumping a well. Keep in mind also that you should shake hands with the interviewer only twice: once at the very beginning of the interview and once as you are going out the door. If the interviewer escorts you out of the employer's offices, a third handshake may also be in order, but use discretion; shaking hands too many times demonstrates insecurity and uncertainty about social protocol.

FOLLOWING UP

When do you send a follow-up letter after an interview, and when do you refrain from doing so? Generally, I send a thank-you note in one of three situations:

1. When the interviewer or the employer has gone out of his way to do me a kindness (such as fly me up to the firm's offices at the firm's expense or give me an autographed copy of his latest book)
2. When I am concerned that something I said during the interview may not be taken the right way, and I wish to clarify my meaning before the interviewer has a chance to screen me out (this only if I am strongly interested in the position)
3. When the interviewer and I have uncovered a special common interest, and I wish to remind him of that common interest (once an interviewer and I discussed a common interest in a little-known music group of the 1960s; the following Sunday I read an article in a local newspaper that one of the group's founders had died suddenly. I sent the interviewer a copy of the article together with a short handwritten

note saying, "Don't know if you saw this—I know you will feel as badly as I do.")

Where you decide a note is appropriate, the note should be short (usually not longer than two paragraphs) and should reiterate your enthusiasm for the position and the interviewer without being unctuous. If possible your note should also remind the interviewer of anything out of the ordinary that you discussed during the interview that will help the interviewer remember you in a positive light (in the case above, I might have said in my follow-up note, "It was good to meet someone else who remembers fondly the XYZ band from the 1960s").

Where the employer is paying certain of your interviewing expenses, it is best to keep the thank-you note separate from the expense account letter in which you seek reimbursement for those expenses. Better still, send the thank-you note to the most important interviewer you met, and send the expense itemization to someone else at the employer—someone less influential—whose job it is to handle such things (like a law firm's recruitment coordinator).

Chapter 5

Some Special Rules for the Luncheon, Cocktail, or Dinner Interview

AT SOME POINT IN your interviewing career, it is inevitable that you will be taken by your prospective employer to a fancy restaurant for lunch, cocktails, and/or dinner. The purpose of such an interview is usually threefold:

1. To give all of the involved parties a treat at the expense of the United States Treasury

2. To see how you handle yourself in a social situation away from the office

3. To get you away from the office in a relaxed setting so that you will be more likely to let your guard down and say some stupid things that will help the interviewers screen you out

You will recall from chapter 1 my interview with Firm A, particularly the part where I was taken to a famous four-star restaurant by a number of the firm's associates. If I had had the benefit of this book when that luncheon interview took place, I would have known a number of things that I did not know then.

First, I would have guessed that the associates were all members of the legal personnel committee and thus were not in a position to "tell tales out of school," even if I hoped in my heart of hearts that they would.

Second, the fact that no partner was present would have alerted me to be on my very best behavior, as I was being led to believe that I could safely let my guard down with a bunch of men and women who, after all, seemed to be my peers in age and experience. Of course, in reality nothing could have been further from the truth; the whole purpose of this exercise was to put me in a position to let my guard down, and that's just what happened.

Finally, I should have been alert to the fact that a boondoggle like this was just as exciting for the young associates (who probably had been slaving until after midnight each night for the preceding month) as it was for me, and I would have known how to turn that to my advantage.

As it turned out, I did not have the benefit of this book. Instead, I went like a lamb to the slaughter, let my hair down, talked incessantly, told every one of my awful war stories, drank way too much, and generally made a bloody fool of myself. As you know, the result was that I did not get an offer from Firm A, but the quickest rejection letter in recorded history (I think they even sent it certified mail to make sure I would get it promptly).

THE MOST IMPORTANT POINT: DON'T RELAX

Lawyers like to think of themselves as social animals, and a large part of their success or failure as professionals depends on how well (or how poorly) their clients perceive them in a social context. People love to be entertained, wined, and dined, just as much as you or I, and every client wants to think of his lawyer as "just a regular person, not that much different than me once he gets out of the office."

Be assured: when you are taken to lunch, cocktails, or dinner, you are being subjected to the most intense scrutiny, as here more than anywhere else you will demonstrate whether or not you are a good fit for that particular firm, corporation, or government agency. I always find these interviews to be the most stressful, in fact, because I cannot rely on my technical skills and hardworking nature to pull me through. In this environment I live or die on my social skills and my ability to deal with people. So DON'T RELAX; you are under a microscope during this interview, and you will have to pull off the performance of your life if you want to get a job offer from these people who are wining and dining you.

THE IMPORTANCE OF CORRECT BEHAVIOR

To survive in a legal job interview, you must develop (if you do not already have them), certain social skills that your years in school and nonlegal jobs have never given you the opportunity to develop. If you are like most people (including me), your education has overlooked a number of social niceties that our forefathers (and sophisticated businesspeople and lawyers who inhabit the society you are about to enter) took for granted.

You have drunk much wine in your time, but you do not know a Bordeaux from a Haut Medoc. You really do not understand what all the forks next to your plate are for. You are not conversant in many of the topics that frequently come up at business luncheons. You do not know how to dance the basic ballroom steps. You do not know the courses in a formal dinner. (Quick! Which comes first, the meat or the fish course?)

This may sound like finishing school stuff to you at first; you may ask yourself, "Are all clients as sophisticated as all that? Won't they appreciate someone who is just one of the guys (or gals)?" Perhaps, but you cannot take that chance. Social conversation among business colleagues or clients is never relaxed and informal. This is not a fraternity house mixer or a brew after work with your old college chums. There is a certain expectation of how you will behave, what you will say, what you will do, and how much you will drink (if you drink at all). You must learn and master the skills necessary to survive in your new setting. In the luncheon interview, as in any other legal job interview setting, you must send the interviewers a signal that you are one of them, that you belong. Following are a few suggestions that will help you get ahead of the competition.

What Do You Talk About?

First, you must be able to carry on a conversation. And not about just anything. For some reason, there are a number of topics that seem to come up again and again during business lunches and other professional social engagements: the current state of the economy (or of a particular industry); the current state of the legal profession; and sports, automobiles, real estate, the performing arts, vacations, and food (including wine).

Subjects that never seem to come up during business lunches (and should be avoided like the plague) include your personal life (especially your romantic activities), shopping, clothes, hobbies that are unrelated to your profession, and scholarly topics. If it is possible to generalize, the topics that come up during business social occasions fall into one of two categories:

1. Topics that demonstrate that the speakers take a broader view of their work than would be apparent if they interacted only at the office.
2. "Safe" topics that demonstrate that the speakers are just normal, everyday folks with the same basic interests as everyone else. If you have never owned a house or a condo in your life and couldn't care less about sports or automobiles, you have much learning to do.

No matter how intensely you work, you simply must find the time to learn what is going on in the world. You must subscribe to a good daily newspaper—one with strong sections on world events, business and the economy, sports, and cultural affairs. When in doubt, there are two standbys: *The New York Times* (traditionally liberal and Democratic) and *The Wall Street Journal* (traditionally conservative and Republican). I would recommend that you have both papers delivered to your home so that you can read them over breakfast or on your way to work; you don't want to clutter up the business day with reading. If you are more oriented toward the Internet, subscribe to the online versions of both newspapers, but make sure you read more than just the headlines and summary paragraphs.

I would also recommend that you subscribe to magazines that offer insights and analysis on the stories you are reading about in your daily newspaper. I personally find the *Economist* to be the best of these; *Time* and *Newsweek,* while they served you well in college and law school, will not be as useful, as they simply rehash the stories from the previous week's daily newspaper. You cannot afford to be more than a day or two out of touch.

If your education on houses, automobiles, cultural matters, or sports is weak, I would recommend subscribing to a publication that treats these subjects in a nontechnical way: *Sports Illustrated,* for example, or *Car and Driver.* Finally, if you know you are having lunch with someone who has a peculiar passion or interest, try to read up on it as much as you can before the luncheon interview so that you can put him at ease and get him to hold forth on something he dearly loves. Who knows? You may even learn something yourself.

This may seem trite to you, but I have found that being able to converse on a variety of topics (especially if they are the right ones for your environment) enhances your self-confidence. Remember that you are not trying to become an expert; your goal, as during a more formal job interview, is to be able to ask intelligent questions, demonstrate to other people that you share their interests, and open up the interviewers so they do as much of the talking as possible.

Rules Regarding Liquor

As for wine and spirits generally, different rules prevail depending on whether the interview is a luncheon, a cocktail session, or a dinner.

For a luncheon interview, the rule is simply stated: DON'T DRINK ANYTHING ... PERIOD. When the waiter asks if you want something to drink, ask for a club soda with lime or a plain tonic water, and don't worry about what the other folks are drinking. No one will question your choice; these days a lot of people are avoiding alcohol altogether, and if anyone does ask, you can always say, "I have a long afternoon ahead of me, and I want to keep a clear head."

If your interview is taking place over cocktails, the general rule is the less exotic, the better. This is not a place for piña coladas, margaritas, or any any other fancy concoction that comes with an exotic or scandalous name. Because it is a cocktail, drink something; if you are uncomfortable drinking alcoholic beverages, try a light beer or a club soda with lime.

If you must drink something alcoholic, my recommendation is Scotch. If you want to impress your interviewer, ask for a specific kind, like Chivas Regal or Dewar's White Label. My experience—based on extensive and thorough research—is that Scotch doesn't go to your head as quickly as other drinks, and even if it does you are unlikely to have a serious hangover the next morning. If you cannot stand the taste of Scotch, try bourbon. It has a sweeter taste, more like brandy. Popular brands are Jack Daniel's and Knob Creek. Avoid asking for any less-refined brands or going by state names (bourbon is often known as Kentucky or Tennessee whisky). These two drinks can be taken on the rocks or with water or soda. Avoid martinis, manhattans, or other such beverages—even if your interviewer is having one—as these are strong drinks that can knock you for a loop even if you limit yourself to one.

A glass of wine or beer is an acceptable drink at a cocktail setting, but is not preferred—especially if you are having dinner with the interviewers immediately afterward. At best, it's unimaginative and at worst, unsophisticated. (Unless, of course, you are interviewing with a firm in northern California that represents a lot of vineyards—in that case do your homework and order a wine from one of the firm's clients.)

Finally, to repeat the point, unless you are interviewing in Honolulu, do not order anything that comes with a little umbrella. If the bar is one that is famous for these, you can always return there after your interviewing is done and indulge to your heart's content.

The Wine List

For a dinner interview, the order of the day (or evening) is wine. I have learned that it helps to know something about wine in the business world. You need not become an expert, but it helps to have more than a rudimentary knowledge of the basics—red wines with meat; white wines with fish or chicken; the lighter the meat's color, the lighter the red wine's taste should be; and never order a white zinfandel.

A useful beginner's guide to the world of fine wines is Kevin Zraly's *Windows on the World Complete Wine Course,* which you will find in paperback at just about any bookstore for under $15. Once you have tasted some of the more common red and white wine labels in Zraly's book, you will usually be able to order from a wine list with confidence.

Another useful book is the *Wine Navigator: Pick the Right Wine Every Time,* by Doug Hexter. You select the type of food, and the *Navigator* tells you exactly what types of wine go with it. Just don't bring the *Navigator* to your dinner interview— look up the wines in advance. Don't be afraid to be a little trendy here. Chianti is the classic matchup for pasta dishes, but a Nero D'Avola from Sicily is just as good and not everyone has heard of it. There are also great resources online: *www.wineanswers.com* has an automated tool for figuring out wine and food pairings.

After a dinner interview, the drink of choice is brandy or cognac. Most people order these by name brand, so it may help if you familiarize yourself beforehand with one or two of the most common brands (such as Courvoisier, Martell, or Remy Martin).

Know Your Way Around the Menu

A luncheon interview, of course, is more than just talk. There is eating and drinking going on as well, and you must have some knowledge of food, wine, and spirits.

When I first started interviewing, I befriended the maitre d' of one of New York's better French restaurants, who for a few dollars on the side walked me through most of the menu items that are staples at French restaurants. He told me which ones the tourists eat, which ones require special utensils (escargot, or snails, usually have to be removed from their shells, and it takes practice to master the special removing tool that the waiter will silently place in front of you with a knowing smile), and which ones should be avoided at all costs (rare, exotic dishes like boiled sheep's brain).

Try to become a connoisseur of as many common cuisines as possible. If you have an interview coming up soon, concentrate on French, Northern Italian, Chinese, and Japanese first, then expand your horizons as time allows. Also, try studying a couple of cookbooks on specific cuisines so that you can understand the menu even better.

What Do You Order?

I will assume that you have done your homework and can identify the dishes on the menu. You should not be ordering anything just because it has a fancy name.

Should you order the most expensive dish on the menu or one of the less expensive specials? Should you order first or after your interviewers have ordered? Should you order what they order? These are questions that will inevitably cross your mind when the waiter comes around to take orders, and there are no easy answers. Let's take them one at a time.

Should You Order the Most Expensive Dish on the Menu or One of the Less Expensive Specials?

This is a tough one. During the heyday of the 1980s on Wall Street, I would have said, "Order one of the restaurant's specialties, even if it is one of the most expensive things on the menu; this will tell the interviewers you are sophisticated and courageous, not easily intimidated, with a hearty appetite for life." In recessionary times, where clients audit every penny of their legal bills, my advice would be not to order the cheapest thing on the menu, but be a little sensitive to price, as the interviewers will not want to hire someone who runs up a client's bill needlessly. In any case, you should order something you like and are comfortable eating; otherwise, you will spend too much time trying to figure out how to eat your entree when you should be focusing on the conversation.

Should You Order First or After Your Interviewers Have Ordered?

I prefer to order after my interviewers have ordered, as this will give me a chance to determine if they are inclined to pinch pennies or go for the gusto, and I then follow their lead with a greater likelihood of success. The trick, of course, is to do this without being too obvious about it. A technique I have used successfully is to not even look at my menu until the waiter approaches the table to take orders, making believe I am totally absorbed in the conversation. When the interviewers ask me if I'd like to order, I say, "You know, I've been so involved I haven't had a chance to even look at the menu. Why don't you go ahead? I'll be ready by the time you're finished ordering." Then, by listening to what is being ordered, I will know how best to fit in with the group.

Should You Order What They Order?

In a word, never. You never order anything one of your interviewers is eating, especially if you are ordering after they have ordered. Doing so demonstrates a lack of imagination, or too great a willingness to follow the crowd. In scanning the menu, you should have a first, second, and third choice, and go with your highest priority that has not been ordered by one of the other persons at the table. If you simply must order something that one of the interviewers is eating, because it is a personal favorite or a world-renowned specialty of that restaurant, try to differentiate your order by asking for a different side dish or (if it is a meat dish) asking to have it cooked differently. Then be sure to tell the interviewers, "I couldn't come to this restaurant and not have this dish!"

If You Are Left-Handed

If you are left-handed, be sure the waiter or maitre d' knows this when you are being seated; at a good restaurant the waiter will know (or will be told) to furnish you with a left-handed table setting. Also, if the table is such that two or more people must sit on the same side, be sure to sit yourself in such a way that there is no interviewer seated to your immediate left. If you fail to do this (and the interviewer to your immediate left is right-handed), your left arm will be constantly poking that interviewer in the ribs.

One Last Point: Neatness Counts!

Just recently I was interviewing a person for a part-time admin position. We went out for lunch at a local Italian restaurant, and he ordered linguini with red sauce. Now, I don't know about you, but I'm the sort of person who can't eat spaghetti without "splattering." Neither could this job candidate.

By the time the lunch was halfway through, there were several dark red stains on the candidate's shirt, and there was at least a half-inch of residual sauce on the candidate's mouth and chin. Aside from the fact that this was not aesthetically pleasing (he looked like an extra in a bad zombie movie), it became obvious that the candidate was totally oblivious to the mess he was making (either that, or he was too embarrassed to clean up in front of me and was trying to bluff his way through it—like I wouldn't notice?). Needless to say, the gross-out factor far outweighed this candidate's background and fit for the job.

At a lunch or dinner interview, never, ever, EVER order something that:

- has a messy sauce;
- must be eaten with your hands; or
- will leave your hands or mouth greasy.

When ordering pasta, stick to penne, rigatoni or other pasta you can pick up with a fork or spoon—anything that has to be twirled should be avoided, especially if red sauce is involved. Preferably, there should be no sauce, or a clear oil-based sauce. And need I say you should avoid anything with garlic like the Plague?

It is extremely hard to look like a modern professional when you're tearing at your barbecued spareribs like a Neanderthal after the kill. If you do, be assured that your interviewer will be 100% focused on the mess you are making and will not even be listening to a word you are saying.

Chapter 6

Negotiating the Tangibles

U P TO NOW WE have been talking about legal job interviews that take place before an offer of employment is
made. The emphasis has been on convincing your prospective employer that you are the best available fit for the job.

Once an offer has been made, there will inevitably be
some discussion of *tangibles* such as salary, pension and
health care benefits, perquisites, and the size and location

of your office. Rarely if ever will these items be discussed in detail prior to a job offer being extended (and you should never, ever, ever bring them up before you have an offer firmly in hand; it signals that you are a money, power, and status grubber who really does not care about the work or the employer's needs).

Once an offer is on the table, however, it is expected that there will be some discussion, and some give-and-take is not only expected but is budgeted for. How much negotiation is sufficient? The answer will of course depend on the job, your employer's willingness to be flexible, and your needs for certain tangibles. There are, however, two rules of thumb that can be stated categorically:

1. The candidate for a job who accepts an offer immediately without any discussion of tangibles is demonstrating his insecurity, his lack of self-esteem, and therefore his unsuitability for the position.
2. The candidate who negotiates too hard and too long over tangibles (especially the less important ones) is demonstrating his unwillingness to follow orders, his inability to become a team player, and therefore his unsuitability for the position.

This is going to be a short chapter, for two reasons. First, this is one of the few areas in which the general, nonlegal books on interviewing skills excel, and you will be well served by looking up one or more of the books listed in the bibliography for guidance in specific situations. Second, and more important for the legal job interviewee, for most legal positions there aren't a whole lot of tangibles available (other than a higher-than-average salary and some prestige), and the employer's room for negotiation is usually quite limited. In a law firm, for example, salary increments are usually based on the number of years a lawyer has spent working since he graduated from law school (and sometimes not even then: at one large law firm in New York City, there are currently four classes of associates who all make the same salary).

What this chapter will do is summarize some of the most important lessons I have learned in negotiating tangibles once a firm job offer has been made.

RULE # 1: "I WANT," NOT "CAN I HAVE?"

When asking for a better tangibles package than the one offered by a prospective employer, the preferred approach is to be polite but assertive. Being too bashful or too mindful of the interviewer's emotional needs at this point in the game will set you back in a big way. The interviewer, who up to now has been totally charmed out of his socks by your presentation, now begins to think you lack the self-confidence necessary to become a successful lawyer (sad but true: a lawyer who is afraid of polite confrontation is not destined to be among the great ones) and may be tempted to reopen the interview to make sure his judgment about you is really correct.

While asking for something more than what is on the table must be done in a way that is consistent with your own style, I believe it is better to do it in the form of declarative sentences describing what you want than to ask for a better tangibles package in the form of a question. For example, let's say a prospective employer has made you an offer at a salary slightly below your expectations. If you respond to the news by saying, "Your offer is most generous, Joe, but do you think it is possible you could go up a few thousand?" your prospective employer may be thinking a number of things:

- "He hasn't really rejected my initial offer. If I say no to this request he'll probably still take it."
- "What makes him think he's worth an extra few thousand? He's just as good as any of our other fifth-year associates, and they don't make anything more than my initial offer."
- "He's made it too easy for me to say no. Do I really want someone like this negotiating multi-million dollar deals for my streetwise clients?"

A better approach might be to say something like, "I think your offer of $70,000 per year is a good one, Joe, but I was hoping for something more in the range of $80,000 in light of my special expertise in this area and my recent stint with the government agency which regulates most of your clients." Here your prospective employer has a tougher time saying no: you have given him a reason to pay you more than other employees who are similarly situated; you haven't really rejected the initial offer, but you have sent a strong signal that your expectations were higher and that the employer should reach a little bit if he wants to get you; and you have sent an even stronger signal that this is an offer you can afford to walk away from (the importance of this will be discussed next under rule 2).

RULE # 2: YOU CAN ONLY GET A BARGAIN ON SOMETHING YOU DON'T REALLY WANT

This advice, incidentally, is from my mother, one of the all-time great flea market hagglers. What it means, simply, is that the more you really want or need something, the less you will risk losing the deal by negotiating aggressively and assertively. You should determine early on if this is a job you really want, a job you would not want under any circumstances, or one which attracts you in a lukewarm way (the job offer will fall in this last category if you find yourself saying, "It's a good job, but there are some negatives, so if I don't get it I won't lose any sleep"). Knowing how much (or how little) the proffered job means to you will largely determine your clout when negotiating the tangibles of the job.

If you have been out of work for a year or more, and someone offers you a job at half your previous salary but enough to pay the grocer and make your mortgage and car payments, you will be hard-pressed to ask for more (even though you may well get more in this situation if you ask for it, as an interviewer is likely to be very impressed by your courage in such a desperate situation). Similarly, if you have been offered a job that nobody but a fool would refuse at a salary that would make anyone green with envy, it will be hard to ask your employer to gild the lily. (Chances are, however, that if you have been made such an offer, it is because you are a very special or unique person who probably can get more if you ask for it because there's only one of you available.) Unless you are very good at bluffing and concealing how much you want or need the position, you will likely end up working on the terms set by your prospective employer.

The converse is also true: the less you want a job, the easier it is to play hardball when negotiating the tangibles (after all, any job is worth doing at the right price). In my last year of college, I interviewed for a sales position with a major radio network. The interviewer, who would have been my boss, dressed in a sharkskin suit, wore an obvious toupee and the loudest tie I had ever seen, used an obvious stage name in his business dealings, and had a faint musty odor about him. Moreover, it soon became clear to me that success in the position would involve incredibly long hours in a very political environment where the prevailing motto was "Sell the customer no matter what you have to tell him," and absolutely no personal contact with customers or other salespeople. Even worse, the opening needed to be filled immediately, so I would have been forced to leave college early, before getting my diploma, to take the job. I decided early on that I was not interested in the position and pushed the interviewer to bring the interview to an end early so that neither of us would waste the other's time.

Well, little did I know that that is the worst tactic to use with an aggressive salesperson; the more I resisted, the more he wanted me for the job. Before I knew it, I had an offer, which I promptly rejected. He then doubled the salary, on the spot. I again said no. The salary went up again. This time I excused myself and left the office; he followed me down the hall and into the street, sweetening the offer. He kept calling me at home, late at night, for three weeks afterward, and each time the salary kept going up until the original offer had quintupled.

By this time, I admit, he was getting close to a number to which I couldn't say no. But he didn't quite get there, and I didn't budge, so eventually he gave up. The moral of the story is that I did not then, and have never since, lost a moment of sleep worrying about what might have happened had I taken the job. It was easy for me to walk away from the situation (contrary to what the salesperson thought,

I honestly did not want the job), and so it was easy for me to negotiate.

RULE # 3: NONCASH TANGIBLES ARE EASIER TO NEGOTIATE THAN CASH TANGIBLES

The first item on anyone's list of tangibles is, of course, salary. Salary is a tangible that requires an employer to fork over cash to you on a regular basis. Cash is scarce, even in good times. What do you do when you and your employer are close to agreement on salary, but it appears that the employer has gone as high as he can go?

There are some very valid reasons why an employer can go only so high on salary and no further. He may only be authorized to go up to a certain figure for the position. If he is to be your future boss, he does not want you making more than he does. If there are others working at the same level for the employer, he does not want your salary to be grossly out of line with theirs (somehow the word always gets out, and it's bad for morale).

When this point has been reached, there are three possible solutions:

1. You cave in and take the last offer on the table.
2. You indicate that you will accept the offer only at the higher salary.
3. You suggest a trade-off.

If you desperately need the job, you go for option 1. If you really don't care whether you get the job or not, you go with option 2. If you are disposed to take the job but not entirely on the employer's terms, you go with option 3.

How do you go about executing option 3? One way is to suggest that while the lower amount can be your base salary, it can and should be supplemented by some sort of incentive compensation based on your performance. That way, your employer is required to pay you the higher amount only if through your efforts there is more money to go around for everybody. This is a common approach for businesspeople whose performance and results can easily be quantified. It is a much more difficult approach for lawyers, whose contribution to an employer is often less tangible. For example, how can you quantify the amount an employer has saved in litigation costs or regulatory penalties because your expert lawyering has prevented it from making a serious and costly mistake?

One possible solution is to negotiate a percentage—over and above base salary—of the firm's receivables from clients that you introduce to the firm. A better approach for legal professionals is to suggest a noncash tangible—one that does not require an immediate or regular outlay of cash—in lieu of the higher salary, such as a window or private office (as opposed to an interior or shared office) or an earlier performance review than would otherwise be the case (the implication here being that the gap between your salary position and that of your employer can be bridged several months hence, when the employer will have a better sense of your value). Or perhaps you can negotiate an extra few days of vacation time or an assurance that you will do a particularly exciting and visible type of work. The key is to want the job enough to be willing to live with the (hopefully temporarily) lower salary.

Generally, this approach is easier when you are interviewing for a corporate job than when you are interviewing for a job with a law firm or a government agency. Law firms are not known for offering a wide variety of benefits. Most of the larger ones view the high salary and prestige of working there as sufficient inducements. A few don't want you to stick around and accordingly have no incentive to make your life at the firm comfortable. The smaller ones are usually so focused on the bottom line that they cannot afford a wide line of benefits. Government agencies are often required by civil service laws to offer the same tangibles—without negotiation—to all applicants for a position at a particular level to avoid discrimination and other undesirable social effects.

RULE # 4: DO YOUR HOMEWORK AND KNOW WHAT IS GETTABLE

How aggressively you negotiate the tangibles will depend to some extent on the relative bargaining power of you and your prospective employer. If you are interviewing for your first legal job with a large and powerful law firm, you will most likely have to take the standard package without much negotiation—unless, of course, you are an editor of the *Harvard Law Review*, graduating first in your class, with a parent who is the chief executive officer of the firm's most important client.

If you have developed a specialty in a hot area of practice and have portable clients who will guarantee $1,000,000 or more in annual billings, and you are interviewing to become partner of a small firm that needs to grow, the balance of negotiating power is quite different; your interviewer may be willing to give you his own office if it means bringing you on board!

Before the tangibles stage of the interview is reached, it is best if you do your homework. Talk to others who occupy similar positions at similar organizations in the same geographic area, and find out what is customary and what is not. This will help you gauge more accurately whether the initial offer is within the ballpark or a lowball that can be improved.

Make sure your requests are realistic and have at least some precedent for the type of organization with which you are interviewing. For example, you would not ask for a company car when interviewing for a law firm; nobody has a company car at a law firm! This can, however, be a negotiable item when interviewing for a corporate legal job.

RULE # 5: REMEMBER THAT YOU ARE STILL INTERVIEWING

Finally, when asking for more than the interviewer is initially willing to give, be sure you give your interviewer good reasons for wanting more. This will help your interviewer justify his concession to himself, his superiors, and his colleagues. Remember that your interviewer is your partner in helping you get what you want, and he will not do this unless he and his organization are simultaneously getting what they want. Keep stressing your unique achievements that make you a better fit for the position than anyone else, your better potential to market the firm to prospective clients, your wealth of connections, your mastery of environmental law, or whatever it takes.

Chapter 7

Strategies for Answering Some Commonly Asked Interviewing Questions

WHEN FRAMING YOUR ANSWER to an interviewer's question, you must first determine the question you are *really* being asked, and then answer the question in a way that both responds to the surface question and furnishes the information the interviewer is really after.

You will have noted by now that I do not believe in form answers for two reasons. First, everyone is different, and a form answer that works for many people may not be convincing in your case. Second, interviewers will be suspicious if your answer sticks too closely to the suggested format. Sadly, there are no easy ways or shortcuts to answering interview questions; you must develop your own, write them down, and make sure you can deliver the words in a sincere, convincing way.

Accordingly, this chapter will not furnish you with form answers, but rather provide an analysis of the interview question and a structure or outline of the right answer that you can then flesh out in your own way. In each case I will try to identify what I think is the hidden question underlying the surface question, and illustrate how I think you can answer both questions with a single answer.

WHY DID YOU DECIDE TO BECOME A LAWYER?

You can expect this question when interviewing for your first job out of law school, although it may crop up for a lateral move or a career change, so you should have an answer prepared just in case.

The question the interviewer is really asking here is: "Did you make this decision with knowledge of what the legal profession is all about, or did you just follow the crowd or let other people make your career decision for you?" In other words, the interviewer wants to know if you are self-directed or other-directed.

No matter what the truth of the situation, you want to provide an answer that shows you are self-directed, that you did your homework before applying to law school, you know what you have gotten yourself into, and you can live with the legal profession's shortcomings. Do not under any circumstances say, "My father (or mother) is a lawyer" or "I didn't know what else to do with myself" or "The law opens up so many different career paths" or "I was attracted by the money and the power," even if these are truthful answers in your case. Similarly, your answer should not be framed as a variation on the theme "I wanted to help other people," as there are many other professions in which that can be done.

Your answer should send the interviewer a strong signal that you wanted to become a lawyer. Your answer should not sound contrived or hokey, but it will go over well if you can give your answer a personal twist (for example, you were attracted by the intellectual stimulation which a legal career affords; you knew a lot of lawyers growing up and were fascinated by their stories of what they did day-to-day; you did a report in grade school on a famous legal case that turned you on to the profession for life).

An answer I have occasionally used when this question is asked goes something like this: "Well, Mr. So-and-So, when I was in college, I knew I wanted a profession that would give me intellectual stimulation, but I couldn't see myself as a college professor; that was too abstract for me. What I love about the law is that it is a scholarly profession, and yet my actions and decisions are having an impact in the real world. I took a couple of legal studies courses in college, and that cemented my decision that this is what I wanted to do with my life."

WHAT COURSES HAVE YOU ENJOYED THE MOST IN LAW SCHOOL?

Again, you can expect this question more when you are interviewing for your first legal job. The question the interviewer really wants to ask is: "What area(s) of practice are you interested in, and will we be able to accommodate your preference(s)?"

You should not answer that you enjoyed courses in an area that is alien to the employer's practice. For example, if your passion is bankruptcy work, you should not bring this up when you are interviewing with a firm that does no bankruptcy work at all. Your research and homework before the interview will give you some idea of the firm's strongest practices, and which ones have the strongest potential for long-term growth. These areas should form the backbone of your answer. If in fact you have not taken any courses in these areas (because, let's say, they are third-year courses and you are interviewing for a second-year summer clerkship), you should say so thusly: "Well, the course I'm looking most forward to is antitrust, but I held off taking it until the third year because the prerequisites for that course are all second-year courses, and I wanted to get these done first."

In your legal career you will have to make a decision fairly early on about whether you will become a litigator handling cases (either at the trial or appellate level) or a legal counselor (such as a corporate lawyer or a trusts and estates specialist) whose practice consists mostly of office work. If you are not careful, this decision will be made for you when you are assigned to your first department within the firm. If you are not sure which approach will give you long-term career satisfaction, your answer should signal your desire to experience both types of practice at the earliest possible time so that you can make an informed decision as early as possible.

WHY ARE YOU LOOKING TO JOIN A [BIG FIRM] [SMALL FIRM] [CORPORATION] AT THIS POINT IN YOUR CAREER?

This question can be asked in almost any interview setting. Your answer must be carefully crafted, because the question the interviewer wants to ask is: "Do you know enough about the different legal environments that I can count on your having a long-term commitment to my employer?"

Interviewers have a general distaste for job hoppers, but they really dislike people who demonstrate that they have not found themselves professionally. Your answer must show some research and should persuade the interviewer that your career horizons are long term. What is more, if you are changing jobs, you must be able to demonstrate why a different environment would be a better fit than your present one.

Your answer to this question will depend on the type of move you are trying to make. If you are looking to switch from a law firm environment to a corporation, for example, you will have to stress a desire to get closer to the business side of things (there are many who think that in-house corporation lawyers do not really practice law at all but are pseudo-businesspeople) and represent one client instead of many.

If you are looking to switch from a corporation to a law firm, your emphasis will be just the opposite: you want to be more of a lawyer, develop expertise in a particular area of practice, and represent a variety of clients instead of just one.

If your move is from a large law firm to a smaller one, you want to stress the desire to work on a variety of matters instead of just a few specialized transactions, and to work on an entire (albeit much smaller) matter from beginning to end rather than working on a very small piece of a very large matter. Your expression of a desire to get closer to the clients and be more of a full-service counselor to them may also be helpful.

If you are looking to move from a smaller firm to a larger one, you will emphasize your desire to become an expert in your field, to experience a greater intellectual challenge, and to deal with new kinds of clients. If you can say it honestly, and if the firm has the reputation for being one of the best in your chosen field, you can say something like, "Frankly, I won't consider myself a successful bankruptcy lawyer until I am working at your firm, because you are the best in the business, and I want to be known as one of the best bankruptcy lawyers around."

If you are interviewing for your first legal job, you can avail yourself of any of the above strategies for answering this question. Interviewers will be most interested in your commitment to a particular geographic area (discussed on pages 13–15), will be somewhat less concerned about your desired area of practice (most large firms will allow you to rotate among several departments in your first few years in practice, and most smaller firms and corporations have a more generalized practice anyway where specialization will be discouraged), and will think it premature for you to be worried about being an expert versus being closer to the business side of things.

WHY DO YOU WANT TO MAKE A CHANGE AT THIS POINT IN YOUR CAREER?

This question is certain to be asked in a lateral-hiring or career-changing situation. Note that this question is the flip side of "What are you looking for in a [small firm] [large firm] [corporation]?" In that case you are being asked to identify the things that interest you in a different environment. In this case you are being asked to identify what you think is wrong about your current environment.

You have to handle this one very carefully; this is a question that should never be answered too honestly or candidly. It's a funny thing about human nature, but when you knock your current employer, you end up knocking yourself much worse in the interviewer's eyes. Nobody (and I mean nobody) likes a whiner or a complainer; every job has its bad days and its negative aspects, and the position for which you are applying is no different.

One of the worst things you can do in a legal job interview is to cite as a negative aspect of your current situation something that the interviewer thinks pertains equally well to the position you are applying for! Your reason for leaving your current employer must be stated in positive terms: it is not so much that your fit with your current employer is not so good, but rather that you see the opportunity for a *much better* fit with the interviewer's employer. How to convince an interviewer that this is in fact so? In particular, how do you do this when in fact you have been fired from your previous employer and are currently unemployed?

First, you should never admit that you are between jobs. If you were fired, talk to your former boss. If the firing was amicable, see if he would be willing to say that you left of your own free will to pursue new opportunities with the old employer's blessing, even though this isn't strictly true. Another positive scenario is that your position was slated for elimination soon, and you expressed a desire to take a look around and see what the market is like right now. The next best scenario is that there was a mutual perception of a less than perfect fit with that employer.

Most bosses will agree to this. Why, you may ask? Because it helps them avoid lawsuits from terminated employees if they play ball to a certain extent. Besides, in a termination situation it is always best for both sides not to burn their bridges behind them. The legal profession is an incestuous one, and no matter how hard you try to avoid brushing up against people you knew professionally in the past, you will be constantly bumping into them—when working on transactions, when sitting on bar association committees, at social functions, and so forth. Who knows? In your next job you may become the world's leading expert in a narrow area of specialization that takes off and becomes the hottest thing since hedge funds. Your old firm may have to refer business to you! In law as in life, excellence is always the best revenge.

Once you have gotten your former boss to agree on the termination story, you are in a much better position to answer the question "Why are you changing jobs right now?" You simply repeat the story that you and your former boss have agreed on.

Let's say you have not been terminated but are simply looking around for a better opportunity. If you are looking at a different legal environment, your answer will track exactly your answer to the question "Why are you looking for a [small firm] [large firm] [corporation]?" Nothing more, nothing less. If you are looking to move to a similar environment in a different geographic location, your answer will track exactly your answer to the question "Why do you want to come to [name of city or town]?" which is discussed below. Nothing more, nothing less. In either case, your answer is framed in terms of what YOU want to do, because of a decision YOU have made.

What if you are looking to move to a similar environment in the same geographic location? In other words, what if you are considering a move to a competing firm or corporation? (I take the view, which some may dispute, that all law firms of a similar size in the same city are competitors.) Your answer to this question will have to include a paean to the superior practice or opportunity for professional development that is available at the new employer, which does not simultaneously knock down your current employer. You may want to say something like, "After working on a variety of matters at Firm P, I have come to the conclusion that I want to make bankruptcy practice my life's work; while Firm P has a pretty good bankruptcy practice, as everyone knows I think the opportunities for bankruptcy lawyers at your firm are much greater, because you are recognized as practicing bankruptcy law at a much higher level than just about anyone in this city."

In all of these situations, you must accentuate the positive and eliminate the negative. What you have is good (or at least you are not unhappy with what you have); what you want is better.

Note that in none of these situations do you give the desire for a lifestyle change as an answer to the question

"Why do you want to change jobs?" You never, ever, ever want to appear burned out in front of a legal job interviewer. Lawyering is hard work, no matter where you practice, no matter what type of law you practice, no matter what your legal environment. The hours are long and unpredictable.

By stressing the need for a lifestyle change, you are in effect answering the question as follows: "I have tried my best to keep up with the demanding pace in my current position, but I just can't do it. I want to slow down, take things easier, have more time for myself, and develop at my own pace." While this may be a totally sincere answer, the interviewer cannot help but think that what you really want is an early retirement or a part-time law practice that will provide the financial security necessary for you to do other things that you find more interesting and challenging. Neither interpretation of your answer will help your cause. You must always appear to the interviewer to be a bright, hardworking go-getter, even if you and he would agree (in a perfect world) that the pace of work at his firm is indeed much slower than it is at your current employer.

The one possible exception (note I say possible) to the rule is where you are a new parent who feels he must adjust his work schedule to perform his child-care duties. There is a growing awareness of the need for flextime in such situations, and some employers (not nearly all, nor even a majority) have begun to enable new parents to reduce their workload during their children's early years, while still being taken seriously as a candidate for advancement and professional development.

I would argue, however, that even in such a situation, where your current employer is not as sensitive to this issue as your prospective new employer would be, you should stress your commitment to the profession and your desire to practice in a different environment that will be a better fit for you. Your status as a new parent can be communicated in other ways, and the message will be received without your having to make it obvious.

WHY DO YOU WANT TO COME TO [NAME OF CITY OR TOWN]?

If you are looking to move to a different geographic area, you will have to explain your reason for moving. You do not want to say that you are following your spouse, even if this is the case. (What if the spouse gets transferred again in a couple of years? Remember that lawyers are looking for long-term commitment.) Nor do you want to say that you want to be closer to a girlfriend or boyfriend (there is no guarantee, after all, that your relationship will be stronger once you are closer together; and besides, giving this as a reason sends a signal to the prospective employer that you value your personal life over your career).

The best reasons for a geographic change are a desire to return to the area where you grew up or went to college or a desire to practice in a location that is world famous for a particular legal specialty that you want to make your own. A specialist in insurance law, for example, would be silly not to consider a stint in New York City or Hartford, Connecticut, where most of the large American insurance companies are based.

In the former case, you are signaling to the interviewer that your roots are strong and that you are unlikely to move from the area once you have settled back in. In the latter case, you are demonstrating a strong commitment to a specialty that is unlikely to move away from that area for a very long time; by moving away from that area, you would be sacrificing much in the quality of your practice.

WHAT WILL YOUR CURRENT BOSS SAY WHEN WE ASK FOR A REFERENCE?

Until you started interviewing, you probably never realized that you would be asked to read someone else's mind. Usually when an employer offers you a job, it is conditioned upon a satisfactory reference from your current boss.

The interviewer who asks this question is looking for you to say something negative about your current boss (which would be a truly stupid thing to do) or to give an assessment of yourself that will prove to be different than what he hears when he calls your current boss for a reference. One way to defuse this question in a harmless way (at least, in a situation where you have not yet had a chance to prepare your current boss for the reference check) is to say something like, "Well, I hope he would say that I was a diligent, hardworking, thorough, and intelligent lawyer, because that's what he has always told me to date." That way, if your boss is foolish enough to say something less enthusiastic about you, it is your word against your boss's word. The interviewer still may choose to take your boss's word over yours, but at least you have not lied outright.

Because of the fear of litigation, most employers are trained never to say bad things about an employee during a reference check. But you can never be sure your boss will know precisely the story you have told your prospective new employer. This is why it is best, in a termination situation, for you to talk with your former employer as early as possible in the process so that you both can get it straight later on (sometimes it is wise to commit the "story" to writing, and make sure you fax a copy to your current or former boss well in advance of a reference check so that he can be prepared). Even where you have not been terminated but have simply accepted a position elsewhere, before you allow your new employer to call your current one, sit down with your current boss and discuss your intentions to leave (only after you have gotten an offer, of course).

A Word about Reference Checks

Many interview books place a lot of emphasis on reference checks and would lead you to believe that a prospective employer would turn you down, even after making you an offer, if your current boss's reference is anything less than an unqualified rave.

In practice, however, it is very hard to tell if someone gives a less than enthusiastic reference because he is genuinely unimpressed by the individual who has worked for him, or he is genuinely upset that such a highly qualified individual is leaving him for employment elsewhere and that he will have to begin the tedious process of replacing him. No interviewer will take the chance that his interpretation of the boss's reference is wrong, thereby saddling him with a possible lawsuit.

Accordingly, when answering this question it is always helpful if you can throw in a comment to the effect that "I suspect my current boss will be extremely upset to hear that

I am leaving; he has been a terrific mentor to me." This will effectively defuse the question, as the interviewer will now have a strong reason to suspect the second interpretation of a less than enthusiastic reference. He will want to believe you, because doing otherwise will either make him doubt his own judgment or compel him to back away from his previous commitment to you (which may cause him embarrassment within the organization).

WHERE DO YOU WANT TO BE TEN (OR FIFTEEN) YEARS FROM NOW?

When an interviewer asks this question, he wants to know if you consider yourself to have the potential for reaching the top ranks of his organization (possibly knocking him out of contention along the way) and whether your career ambitions are realistic.

An incorrect, although possibly sincere answer to this question would be: "I want to be a partner in your firm. Period." Ten or 15 years is a long time, after all, and people's goals and expectations change over that long a period of time; I think an interviewer would perceive such an answer as immature.

Another incorrect answer would be: "Who knows? Ten or 15 years is a long time; I believe in going with the flow." Everybody has to have some goals in life, after all. I mean, if you don't plan on going anywhere, how do you know which way to go? How do you know that you really want to be a lawyer, if that is how you feel about things? I think an interviewer would perceive this answer as indicating a lack of goal-setting ability, ambition, and drive. Generally, Type B people (people who are relaxed, calm, and take each day as it comes) tend not to do well in legal environments, where Type A personalities (intense, driven, inclined to push themselves and those around them as hard as they can) tend to succeed in the long run.

In answering this question you should appear to be ambitious but realistic. A useful strategy is to cast it in the form of "I want to be working in an environment that will make me happy," with the clarification that at least right now you think the interviewer's employer is such an environment. For example, you might want to say something like, "I want to be practicing in an environment where I am constantly stimulated and challenged by the quality of the work and where I can be a recognized expert in my chosen field of bankruptcy law; as your firm is recognized nationwide for the quality of its bankruptcy work, I would hope you would still want me around after all that time, and I think it's an environment that would make me very happy."

Note that you have not said you want to be a partner; you have merely said that you want to be there still, doing the work you love. That's the kind of answer lawyer/interviewers like: one that demonstrates your long-term commitment to a line of work, but one that does not require a reciprocal commitment from the employer.

Keep in mind that your answer to this question must be tailored to the legal environment for which you are interviewing. The answer I have suggested above would not work with a smaller law firm, a government agency, or a corporate legal department.

DO YOU HAVE ANY HOBBIES OR OUTSIDE INTERESTS?

Beware! This question is a trap! In asking this question, the interviewer wants you to relax and tell him about all the things you love to do outside your work that you will no longer have any time to do once you start practicing law! I think this is probably the most dangerous screening-out question an interviewer can ask, and you should approach it with kid gloves.

Above all, do not view this question as signaling the interviewer's sincere interest in your personal life. What he wants to hear is that you are just as much of a dull stick as he is, and therefore a perfect fit for his employer. The correct answer will signal two things to the interviewer: you really don't have many interests outside of your work, and the few interests you do have will help make you a better lawyer.

You might, for example, want to say something like, "Well, most of my time is tied up with work, and my family obligations take up most of the rest of my time. I do, however, love to read, and I play golf whenever I can." This tells the interviewer you will have few distractions from your work life, and the few distractions you will have are things of which he can approve. A good golf game will help you cement relationships with clients, and your work will involve more than a little bit of reading—just don't admit to reading the Harry Potter novels, as a healthy imagination is not always considered a positive attribute in a good lawyer. If the interviewer asks you what you like to read, say history or biography or something else that shows your serious, logical, nonfrivolous side.

HOW WOULD YOU DESCRIBE YOUR STRENGTHS?

I have to believe that this question and its companion, "How would you describe your weaknesses?" are asked during 99 percent of the legal job interviews conducted in the United States this year. You are virtually certain to be asked these two questions, so there is absolutely no excuse for you not to have an answer prepared in advance. One of the surest ways to screen yourself out in a legal job interview is to signal to your interviewer that these questions are coming as a surprise to you.

When the interviewer asks this question, he is looking to hear about things that directly relate to the practice of law in his particular environment and that he can use to sell you to his colleagues on the legal personnel committee or to the other lawyers in the corporate legal department. An inappropriate answer would be: "Well, I once chugged 15 consecutive cans of beer during a fraternity house party in college, so I guess you could say I hold my liquor well." While this may satisfy the interviewer's second criteria, it does not help him with the first.

A better answer can be structured something like this: "I love the intellectual challenge of the law, for the same reason I think I have always loved puzzles, games, and mysteries of all kinds. I get so absorbed when I'm working on a problem that I totally lose track of time and cannot rest until I am comfortable I have the solution. I also have extremely strong people skills and can get along with just about anybody. But most importantly, I know that (even though I have been doing this for a few years now) there is still a lot to learn, and probably always will be; I am not the sort of person ever to take my knowledge for granted."

This tells the interviewer that you are detail oriented, are willing to do the work involved in finding a solution (note that I did not say, "I cannot rest until I am comfortable I have found the answer"—finding the answer may be only the first step in solving a client's problem), and will not turn people (especially clients) off with your personality or bad habits. Finally, you have signaled your maturity (the law is always changing, and it is impossible to know everything there is about any area of practice) and humility in considering yourself a perpetual student of the law, one who does not shoot from the hip because he thinks he knows it all.

WHAT DO YOU CONSIDER YOUR MOST SERIOUS WEAKNESSES?

This is probably the only interview question in which the surface question and the real question are one and the same, and the only one you can take at face value. While this is probably the most dreaded question in any job interview, it is surprisingly easy to answer. When the interviewer asks this question, he hopes you will be naive enough to actually volunteer that you have weaknesses! Yet it would not be the right answer to say, "Well, I've given this a lot of thought, and I really can't think of any." Everybody has weaknesses; a failure to admit that is a sign of immaturity. How to answer this question without volunteering any weaknesses?

The key in answering this question is that what constitutes a weakness is simply a matter of perception. What you consider a personal weakness others may perceive as your strongest attribute. All you need to do when answering this question is to avoid mentioning anything that the interviewer perceives as a weakness and can use as the reason for screening you out. To put it differently, to answer this question correctly you must list one or two traits (never any more than that) that the interviewer is highly likely to regard as strengths, regardless of whether you actually view them as weaknesses.

You might, for example, want to say something like, "Well, a lot of people think I have an unbalanced life because I spend so much time on my work, and there are times I wish I could develop some more outside interests, but I take my work very seriously so that's awfully hard for me to do. As for other weaknesses, I guess you could say that I'm an impatient sort of person; I push myself very hard, and I sometimes get a little concerned when things aren't happening and there isn't much to do. I have to be busy or else I'm not happy."

Tell me, what weaknesses have you demonstrated by this answer? Only that you are a hard-charging workaholic with few outside interests and a desire to get things done. Guess what? As a successful lawyer, your interviewer shares these very weaknesses—they are the very things (being intensely focused, having few distractions from the outside world, pushing himself hard to meet client deadlines and get the results the client wants) that have made him successful. There is no way he will view these attributes as weaknesses, so you have accomplished your task.

Of course, you must be able to say this sincerely and with feeling. Your acting ability counts for much here; if your interviewer thinks you are merely spewing out an answer you read in an interview book somewhere, it is all over for you, so make yours as original as possible while still keeping to the traditional "nonweakness weakness" theme. There are some interviewers who actually look for the traditional answer as a sign that you know what's going on in the world: I once had an interviewer tell me, "You know, Mr. Ennico, everybody gives that answer, and you know what? It's the only right answer to that question! Any other answer and you would blow yourself out of the water. You pass the 'stupid question' test; now let's get down to business."

HERE'S A SITUATION I'M WORKING ON RIGHT NOW IN THE OFFICE. WHAT WOULD YOU DO IF YOU WERE IN MY SHOES?

This is probably the most stressful question you can be asked during a legal job interview. The interviewer appears at first blush to seek proof of your technical competence. Actually, in cases where the interviewer is not seeking free legal advice, he has a much different agenda. What he really wants to know is either how you go about analyzing a difficult situation when it is first presented to you, much as a client would present it to you, or how you handle a tough question when you know (and the interviewer knows) that you don't have the correct answer on the tip of your tongue. Will you bluff your way through and risk annoying the interviewer (or the client)? Will you take an educated guess and risk a malpractice lawsuit? Will you admit you don't know the answer and risk losing the client's confidence and trust? This question is full of potential land mines.

There is no one way to handle this type of question, but unless it is a situation you have encountered before and you know the answer right off (in which case you should not hesitate to demonstrate your expertise), the better approach is not to answer the question at all but show how you would go about finding the answer in a way that demonstrates you are thorough, cautious, and not inclined to shoot from the hip under pressure.

I would begin by listening carefully to the facts given by the interviewer and asking a couple of clarifying questions before putting together an answer. This shows your ability to focus on the important points—the operative facts in the interviewer's hypothetical situation—and filter out the irrelevant details, while also demonstrating to the interviewer that you do not rush to decisions.

If you are interviewing for your first job out of law school, and you really don't know anything about the area of law that applies to the interviewer's situation, your answer at this point is an easy one: "Mr. So-and-So, I can see that an answer to this question thoroughly requires a knowledge of XYZ law, which is a course I have not yet taken, although I intend to [or "which we covered in my first-year property course, and which I remember in a general way only"]. I would obviously not want to speak precipitously and would want to familiarize myself thoroughly with this area of the law or seek help from other lawyers in the firm who specialize in this area, before attempting a definitive answer, certainly before giving the client advice on which he is going to rely."

If you are applying for a lateral position or are seeking a career change, and if you have held yourself out as having some experience or expertise in the law relevant to the interviewer's question, you will have to take a stab at it. Once you have gotten all of the information you feel you need to attempt an analysis, I would begin by saying, "Of course, this is not the kind of question that has a hornbook answer. To give a definitive answer, first, I would want to know more about [certain facts that have legal consequences]. Then, I would want to refresh myself on certain fine points of the law in this area, particularly [one or two statutes or leading cases that bear directly on the issues in question]. Finally, I would need to know how the legally correct answer would go over with the client politically; if I had not had any contact with the client directly, I would want to talk to other lawyers in the firm who have. If you put a gun to my head, though, and told me I had to answer on the spot, I would say that the client is taking a serious legal risk in doing what he proposes to do, and I would advise him against taking further action until we could furnish him with a more studied answer."

This answer may not be totally satisfying, but it will answer the interviewer's real question of how you solve problems. Note especially that I took into account not only the need for a correct legal analysis, but also the need to tailor the answer to the client's political situation. This usually will impress a lawyer/interviewer, whose primary job is to keep his clients happy and in compliance with the law, not necessarily to find legally correct answers that nobody can use.

SUMMARY

Because this is such an important subject, I think it is useful to review some of the most important points about answering an interviewer's questions during a legal job interview:

- Always look for the hidden question lurking beneath the surface question, and be sure to provide the information the interviewer is really looking for.

- Preparation is everything; in an ideal situation there should be no question which you have not anticipated in advance.
- Always tailor the answer to your interviewer's situation; your answers must always demonstrate a fit with the legal environment and culture of that particular employer, and must show the interviewer that deep down you are the same sort of person as he is.
- Never volunteer negative information about yourself.
- Never indicate that a question has surprised you or caught you unaware.
- Keep your answer short, concise, and to the point.
- Remain silent after you have given your answer; if an uncomfortable silence ensues and the interviewer does not pick up the conversation, ask a follow-up question or one of your pre-pared questions.
- Never relax or let your guard down, especially if the question is a seemingly harmless one about your outside interests.
- Don't fudge an answer; if you don't know, try to buy time to find the right answer, or (in the case of a technical legal question) tell the interviewer what you would do and what you would need to know in order to come up with an answer that works.

Chapter 8

A Final Thought: The Good Interviewee Never Stops Interviewing

THIS BOOK IS ABOUT the legal job interview, but if there is one thing I would want every reader to take away from this book, it is that interviewing skills are part of your everyday life and work as a lawyer.

When people talk about a lawyer counseling a client, what do they mean? What else if not an interview, where the lawyer (interviewer) is trying either to persuade the client (candidate) that he should take or refrain from taking certain action because of the legal consequences involved, or to elicit information from that client that will help the lawyer find the legally correct solution? Perhaps this is why the clinical legal studies course in client handling, which is offered at just about every law school in the United States, is invariably called Interviewing and Counseling.

Interviewing skills are not put on the shelf once you receive a job offer. The same techniques that are necessary to impress a lawyer/interviewer favorably are the same techniques necessary to win over a client or colleague who, for various motives, may have just as much reason to try to screen you out as a lawyer/interviewer who must pick a winner out of a hatful of qualified candidates.

The good interviewee never stops interviewing; he hones and polishes his skills to a fine gloss, makes mental notes or written files of recurring interview situations, and forever seeks to come across in the light most favorable to himself, while focusing all of his concentration and energy on making the other guy open up, do all the talking, and maybe make a mistake or two.

There is a saying in Zen Buddhism: "You cannot pour water into a cup that is already full." What is meant is that you cannot learn anything by reading something written by someone else or listening to what someone else has to say, when you are focused on the thoughts whirring around your head (the Zen Buddhists also say, "The mind is like a drunken monkey"). One of the first lessons in any speed-reading course is to stop verbalizing in your mind the words that you read on the printed page—to let your eyes scan the words quickly without anything happening between your ears. Amazingly, you retain the information better this way than by reading each word and sounding it out in your head.

To truly absorb information from the outside world, you must quiet yourself internally, literally turn yourself off like a lightbulb, so that you can not only catch the words and pictures coming in from without, but also feel the rhythm and the music—the tone of voice and body language of the person speaking, the context in which he places information—that in the end may tell you more about the other person and what he is trying to tell you than the words themselves.

This process of turning yourself off and focusing the interview on the other person lies at the heart of successful legal job interviewing. I respectfully submit that it lies at the heart of the lawyer's life and work as well.

Good luck! And remember:

- You already have the job
- Warm, friendly, smile, low-key
- Calm, confidence, courage, control
- Don't volunteer any negatives about yourself
- SAY AS LITTLE AS POSSIBLE

Bibliography

IF YOU ARE AT all familiar with career books in general, you know that they inevitably contain a chapter or two on interviewing, usually with some sample questions and answers. Without overlooking any of these efforts, some of which are quite good, I thought it would be helpful to list some of the books currently available in bookstores that focus their attention on interviewing techniques and strategies.

Keep in mind that these books do not discuss interviewing for a legal job and tend to be quite general in their outlook. Nonetheless, you may pick up some clever answers to some of the more routine questions that legal interviewers will ask (if for no other reason than that they've read the same books) and perhaps one or two more tips about dress and body language (about which, frankly, you cannot read too much). Finally, just because a book is listed here does not mean I endorse it or have even read it.

Books on Interviewing

How to Turn an Interview into a Job (Completely Revised and Updated), by Jeffrey G. Allen. Published by Fireside Books/ Simon & Schuster, Inc. Available in paperback for $11.95. First published in 1983 and still in print today! Anything by Jeffrey G. Allen on this topic is worth reading.

The Five-Minute Interview: A New and Powerful Approach to Interviewing, by Richard H. Beatty. Published by John Wiley & Sons, Inc. Available in paperback for $24.95.

Your First Interview, by Ron Fry. Published by Career Press. Available in paperback for $11.99.

The 250 Job Interview Questions You'll Most Likely Be Asked, by Peter Veruki. Published by Adams Media Corporation. Available in paperback for $9.95.

General Books on Legal Career Management

The Lawyer's Career Change Handbook: More Than 300 Things You Can Do With a Law Degree (Updated and Revised), by Hindi Greenberg. Published by Avon Books, Inc.

Nonlegal Careers for Lawyers, Fifth Edition, by Gary A. Munneke. Published by the American Bar Association.

What Can You Do with a Law Degree? A Lawyer's Guide to Career Alternatives Inside, Outside & Around the Law, by Deborah Arron. Published by DecisionBooks.

Business Lawyer's Handbook: A Guide to the Corporate Lawyer's Life and Work, by Cliff Ennico. Self-published by author.

Audiobooks
Your Legal Career: Finding Success and Satisfaction in the American Legal Profession, by Cliff Ennico. Self-published by author.

Websites
You can get a lot of great information on the Web, but advice on interviewing for a legal job is hard to find. Many legal recruiters offer career advice on their websites, but the advice is best taken with a ton of Morton's finest. Here are some of the least biased/most helpful sites:

- *www.law.com/jsp/law/careercenter/advice.jsp*—the careers page of the *National Law Journal's* website
- *www.lawjobs.com*—the careers website for *The American Lawyer* and its related publications
- *www.nalp.org*—the website of the National Association for Law Placement in Washington, D.C.
- *www.legalcareer.com*—the website for Cliff Ennico's legal career management publications, blogs, and views on career opportunities in the American legal profession

Index